THE
DYMOCK POETS

(5)

The Soldier.

If I should die, think only this of me:
That there's some corner of a foreign field
That is for ever England. There shall be
In that rich earth a richer dust concealed;
A dust whom England bore, shaped, made aware,
Gave, once, her flowers to love, her ways to roam,
A body of England's, breathing English air,
Washed by the rivers, blest by suns of home.

And think, this heart, all evil shed away,
A pulse in the eternal mind, no less
Gives somewhere back the thoughts by England
given,
Her sights and sounds; dreams happy as her day;
And laughter, learnt of friends; and gentleness,
In hearts at peace, under an English heaven

fr. 'The Soldier' by Rupert Brooke, written by him on Battalion notepaper

THE
DYMOCK POETS

Sean Street

Border Lines Series Editor
John Powell Ward

seren

Seren is the book imprint of
Poetry Wales Press Ltd
Wyndham Street, Bridgend, Mid Glamorgan

British Library Cataloguing in Publication Data

Street, Sean
Dymock Poets. — (Border Lines Series)
I. Title   II. Series
821.91409

ISBN 1-85411-121-3 hbk
1-85411-122-1 pbk

*The publisher acknowledges the financial support of the
Arts Council of Wales*

Cover illustration:
Outside the Birmingham Repertory Theatre, 1914:
Drinkwater, Gibson, Edward Marsh, Abercrombie

Printed in Palatino by WBC Book Manufacturers, Bridgend

Contents

List of Illustrations

A Dymock Chronology

THE DYMOCK POETS

1912   Robert Frost and family arrive in Britain (September)
Brooke meets Wilfrid Gibson (September)
Publication of *Georgian Poetry 1911-1912* (October)

1913   The Poetry Bookshop officially opened (January)
Birmingham Repertory Theatre opens (February)
A Boy's Will by Robert Frost published (April)
Alfred Austin dies (June). Succeeded as Poet Laureate by Robert Bridges
Gibson meets Frost (August)
Edward Thomas meets Frost (October)
Gibson marries Geraldine Audrey Townshend, and they move into 'The Old Nailshop'

1914   *New Numbers 1* published (February)
The Frosts move to Little Iddens, Ledington
In Pursuit of Spring by Edward Thomas published (April). Thomas visits Frost at Ledington
New Numbers 2 published (April)
Rebellion by Drinkwater first performed, Birmingham Rep. (May)
North of Boston by Frost published (May)
Rupert Brooke returns from overseas (June)
Thomas visits Frost at Ledington
Archduke Ferdinand assassinated, Sarajevo (28 June)
New Numbers 3 published (August)
Edward Thomas and Merfyn set off for holiday with the Frosts (2 August)
Germany invades Belgium, British ultimatum to Germany ignored. War declared (4 August)
Helen Thomas and children travel to Ledington by train (5 August)
Eleanor Farjeon travels to Ledington (20 August)
Thomas and family and Eleanor Farjeon leave Ledington (September)
Rupert Brooke enlists (September)
Abercrombies leave 'The Gallows' to travel. The Frosts move to 'The Gallows' (September)
Rupert Brooke involved in Antwerp action (October)

Edward Thomas writes first poem ('Up in the Wind'), visits Frost at Ryton (November)

1915   Brooke completes '1914' sonnet sequence (January)
New Numbers 4 published (January)
First poems published by 'Edward Eastaway' — 'Horse and Man' and 'Interval' — in *Root and Branch* no.4; 'Haymaking' and 'The Manor Farm' in *This England*
Eleanor Farjeon stays with the Frosts at 'The Gallows' (January/February)
The Frosts sail from Liverpool for USA (13 February)
Brooke sails from Bristol for Dardanelles (28 February)
Brooke dies, buried on Skyros (April)
1914 and Other Poems by Brooke published (June)
Thomas enlists in the Artists' Rifles (14 July)

1916   Abercrombie undertakes industrial war work in Liverpool (April)
Gibson leaves for reading tour of USA (October)
Six Poems by Edward Eastaway published (Pear Tree Press)

1917   *An Annual of New Poetry* published (March)
Edward Thomas killed (9 April)

1923   Lascelles Abercrombie delivers Clark Lectures, Cambridge

1925   *Collected Poems* by Wilfrid Gibson published (Macmillan)

1928   Frost visits England

1930   *The Poems of Lascelles Abercrombie* published (O.U.P.)

1937   Death of John Drinkwater

1938   Death of Lascelles Abercrombie

THE DYMOCK POETS

1957   Frost visits England for the last time (May/June)

1962   Death of Wilfrid Gibson

1963   Death of Robert Frost

1965   Death of Eleanor Farjeon

1. Dymock, Place and Time

For a brief time in the months that always seem to have been golden before the First World War, the little village of Dymock in Gloucestershire was a lively centre of literary activity. Major names from the world of literature came and went, poets walked its fields and lanes, and literary futures were shaped. Writers with international reputations lived here, and poems and prose celebrating its landscape were written that have since found their way into books and anthologies around the world. A respected Georgian journal was published, literally as a cottage industry, and men and women sought an idyll of Dream England, as if they knew that this, perhaps, might be their last chance. Lascelles Abercrombie, Wilfrid Gibson, Edward Thomas, Robert Frost, John Drinkwater, Rupert Brooke...these were the Dymock poets, but there were others who came here to visit; Edward Marsh, founder of the Georgian movement, Eleanor Farjeon, W.H. Davies, Ivor Gurney, and many more. Dymock saw a coming together that at the outset did indeed seem to those involved like an idyll, something almost perfect, writers working with one end in view, supporting one another, sharing experience, all in a beautiful landscape. It must have seemed as though it was too good to last. And it was.

Dymock has always been a place where people and landscape come together. A place where in crossing a field you can move into another county, and where on the right spring day at daffodil time the early sunlight touching pasture can produce a response that recalls an instinct for essences we thought we had left behind in childhood. A place of curlews and cuckoos in their season, and a heavy red loamy soil that has bred flowers and fruit trees, and supported agriculture since pre-Roman times. A place about which the eighteenth century Gloucestershire historian Samuel Rudder

11

wrote at blossom time:

> It has been compared to a garden overspread with flowers;
> but the utmost stretch of verbal description would produce
> an idea very inadequate to the beauty of this flowery land-
> scape.

The village of Dymock lies thirteen miles north-west of Gloucester
and four miles south of Ledbury. Together with the hamlets of
Preston and Kempley it occupies the north-west corner of Gloucestershire, pressing gently against Herefordshire and Worcestershire.
Indeed, apart from Yorkshire, Gloucestershire itself touches more
counties than any other in England. At Dymock, turning a full 360
degrees, the eye takes in not one landscape but many. The Malvern
Hills loom to the north, and their last outcrop, May Hill to the south,
is a strange hill, low and yet somehow always dominating the
skyline, pulling from the earth like a great smooth whale, and
crowned by a circlet of trees. It is a land of rich variety, and the fields
of Dymock give the village a topography of its own, gentle, yet
always with the potential to change character at the turn of a corner,
and make one gasp.

The name has had many variations, from Denimock to Dymoke
with at least twelve other alternatives in between, and there are
almost as many possible explanations of its meaning. It could for
instance derive from the Saxon words Dim (obscure) and Aac (Oak)
— a place in the shelter of oaks. It has been suggested on the other
hand that it comes from a corruption of the Welsh, Tŷ (house) and
Mocher (Swineherd). Yet another derivation has been suggested by
J.E. Gethyn-Jones, an assiduous chronicler of the village's history,
who has linked the name to a lost Roman town on the site, Macato-
nium. Following this line of thought we could contrive Dim, (ob-
scured or obliterated) and Mac, (being an abbreviation of the Roman
name).

Setting aside such gentle controversy, it is certainly clear that
Dymock is an ancient place, and that it was once much bigger and
more commercially important than it is today. Clinging as it does for
a few hundred yards to the B4215 road out of Newent, the village
itself might not repay the idle glance of the passing motorist with
stunning vistas of picture-book rural architecture. But it has its
moments, with some fine thatched cottages, and a rich mix of period

houses, and the Church of St Mary with its little green is a delight. Once the road has shaken the village off, it opens itself up to the straight certitude of the old Roman road, whose line it follows on to Hope under Dinmore near Leominster.

On either side of this road lies the Dymock countryside, mottled with tiny hamlets that punctuate the landscape, and which form reference points for the visitor. To the east is Ryton, to the north, on the Ledbury Road, the crossroads called Greenway, and slightly to the north-west again is Ledington. West of this little community, over rolling meadows, is Preston, and south of there, Kempley, with its ancient church containing the most perfect Saxon wall paintings in existence anywhere in the world. There are other places, such as Much Marcle with its spectacular churchyard yew, and placenames like Tiller's Green and Hay Traps which tell you something of the working past. Through it all runs the River Leadon, winding down from Ledbury with the Malverns beyond, rustling through the red-soil countryside and enriching the already verdant land.

Dymock is a place where people live, rather than a self-conscious image selling itself to tourists. But it was once much bigger, a town in the Middle Ages with all the rights of fairs and a market; many historians from the late eighteenth and early nineteenth centuries speak of lost houses, and a disappeared thriving rural community, for which one of the main industries was the wool trade.

Dymock was always, then, a practical place where the business of life has not allowed over-indulgence in the beauty of the landscape that surrounds it. For it is in that very landscape that Dymock's glory is to be found; a working beauty, functional in that the natural propensities of nature to create itself have been fostered; in other words, a partnership. The wild daffodils that have for so long been a wonder of the place — inevitably less so today than in the past because of modern farming methods — were cultivated as a crop in medieval times, when they were harvested to make dye for hessian and cloth. The same was true of blackberries in the area. Later, in the nineteenth century and into the twentieth, the daffodils were sold as flowers rather than for their pigment, with a large market in London and elsewhere, and pickers came from all over the country at harvest time. It was a major industry. And, although this too has dwindled, part of the landscape has always been given over to cider orchards; in 1714, Wantner in his *History of Gloucestershire* stated:

> Dimock and Kempley...are two of the most noted parishes in
> England for making the most and best Rare VINUM DIMO-
> CUUM or that transcendent Liquor called RED-STRAKE
> SIDER not much inferior to the best French Wines.

*

Dymock has produced some significant personalities, among them
the great ecclesiastic Roger Dymock or Dimmock, well known for
being a central figure in the convocation of Oxford doctors who
attacked the theses of John Wycliffe in 1382. The village can also
boast the birthplace of the great seventeenth century philanthropist
and countryman, John Kirle, 'The Man of Ross', who was christened
in St Mary's Church on 4 June 1637. It is fitting that such a guardian
of rural beauty should have been born here.

But Dymock — like many country communities in the past — has
known the darker side of superstition. In 1892, a small lead tablet
was found. The tablet, dating from the seventeenth century, bore an
inscription which has become known as the Dymock Curse. It is a
charm invoking the names of spirits against one Sarah Ellis "to make
this person to banish away from this place and countery [sic] Amen
to my desier Amen". Who Sarah Ellis was is not known, nor why she
should incur such wrath. But local legend has it that she was driven
demented by knowledge of the curse, and took her own life. She was
buried at a crossroads in Dymock Woods with a stake driven
through her body at a site which became known as 'Ellis's Cross'.
Notwithstanding this gruesome tale, Dymock was apparently re-
nowned for its friendliness. Rudder, writing in the late eighteenth
century, claimed:

> Dimmock was ever remarkable for hospitality. The Lords of
> the Manors and other proprietors of the best estates used to
> reside in the parish and their houses were open to all comers;
> and though some have now left it, yet the same convivial old
> English spirit remains with this generous hospitable people.

Be that as it may, it has not been unusual for rural communities to
look questioningly at unexplained newcomers, especially in times of
national strife. A group of people claiming to be poets, some with
curious accents, coming into this landscape and wandering its lanes
with no apparent purpose just as the clouds were gathering prior to
the First World War, must be expected to run the gauntlet of some

local suspicion. With no apparent jobs to do, not observing the rhythms of the countryside in their day-to-day activities, how could it be otherwise?

*

Yet Gloucestershire has bred its share of poets, many of whom have sung their song quietly, not seeking to court publicity, and who have consequently gone largely unheard. For instance the Victorian poet Sydney Dobell, living chiefly at Hucclecote and Nailsworth, wrote some interesting lyrics, although he tended to obscure his talent with his unfocused indulgence in a rather formless outpouring. Others achieved more fame: W.H. Davies, Ivor Gurney, and James Elroy Flecker, "born a Londoner and bred in Gloucestershire" to quote his own words. The county echoes through many of his poems, often when we least expect it:

> November evenings damp and still
> They used to cloak Leckhampton Hill
> And lie down close on the grey plain
> And dim the dripping window-pane
> And send queer winds like Harlequins
> That seized our elms for violins.

The eastern Cotswolds provided the setting for many of the poems of Wilfred Rowland Childe, epitomised by such as 'Dream Cotswold':

> Moreton, Bourton and Stow, Marsh, Water and Wold,
> Where none grow weary at all and none grow old,
> Where the trees have emerald leaves and the streets are
>   gold.

John Freeman, at Weston Subedge on the border of Gloucestershire and Warwickshire, once wrote of his own work that "there is a good deal of that country lying about visibly or just below the surface in my poems". Likewise these two counties will argue over the work of the late nineteenth century poet Norman Gale, although at his best it was the Cotswold scenery that he described most vividly. Markus Rickards of Twigworth, Gwynne Evans of Woodchester, Sidney Harland of Gloucester, Cyril Winterbotham and Adam Lindsay Gordon of Cheltenham and F.W. Harvey of Minsterworth are all names to be included in any rollcall of the area's literature. Today, John Taylor 'The Water Poet', who plied a ferryman's trade on the Severn, is too much neglected. Later he transferred himself to the Thames, and wrote long poems about both rivers.

W.E. Henley was born and educated in Gloucester, and was noted for — among other things — a strong friendship, abruptly terminated, with Robert Louis Stevenson. The two men had met while Henley was in hospital, recovering from the amputation of a tubercular foot. He had written a sequence of sonnets, 'In Hospital', which were published in the *Cornhill Magazine*, and Stevenson had asked to meet him. On his recovery Henley — a man of flowing red hair and beard — was determined not to be cowed by his disability, and perhaps over-compensated. He once knocked Oscar Wilde over with his crutch, and in May 1883, Stevenson confessed in a letter: "It was the sight of your maimed strength and masterfulness that begot John Silver in Treasure Island". So many names, some familiar, many obscure, peopled this corner of England. Names like John Philips, 'The Cider Poet', who lived from 1676-1708:

> Be it thy choice when Summer heats annoy
> To sit beneath her leafy canopy
> Quaffing rich liquids, Oh! How sweet to enjoy
> At once her fruits and hospitable shade.

And to step again over a county border into Herefordshire is to come to Hope End, where Elizabeth Barrett spent much of her childhood and youth on her father's 475 acre estate. Just under two miles north of Ledbury, and four miles south-west of Malvern, it was home to her from the age of three, in 1809, until 1832, when her father was forced to sell it. Many of her early poems were inspired by the district, including 'The Lost Bower', which was set in the wood above the house. Later, in a letter to Miss Mitford, she recalled her feelings when the house was opened to auction, and "our old serene green stillness was trodden under foot". And the place continued to echo in her poetry:

> Hills, vales, woods settled in silver mist
> Farms, granges, doubled up amongst the hills
> And cottage chimneys smoking from the woods.
> And cottage gardens smelling everywhere,
> Confused with smell of orchards.

And of course the Ledbury-born John Masefield could not escape the influence of the neighbouring topography. 'Reynard the Fox' races through the Herefordshire and Gloucestershire countryside. Masefield — himself christened at Preston church — allows a christening party in that very place to see the fox as he runs. 'The Daffodil Fields' were a part of his childhood, known as they were then as "The Hall House Meadows", and the closing pages of *The Everlasting Mercy* contains images of the Dymock area, some of which puzzled early readers of the poem:

> I've marked the May Hill ploughman stay
> There on his hill, day after day
> Driving his team against the sky,
> While men and women live and die.

Later, in an essay on his childhood landscape, he explained the image:

> In early childhood, I often saw the heave of May Hill, possibly twelve miles to the SSW. On its summit, at that time, there was a big, scattered clump of old well-grown and wind-smitten pine-trees. Time, the axe, and possibly picnic-parties' fires, had dealt strangely with these trees, so that from anywhere near Ledbury, especially from near the Bullen Coppice on the road to Gloucester, they looked exactly like a giant ploughing with a team... Sometimes, when men were burning weeds, leaves, old grass, gorse, or hedge-clippings on that distant hill, he seemed to be ploughing fire...

Masefield, born in 1878, was perhaps articulating what he saw as a child of the May Hill profile before 1887, when a fresh set of pines was planted to celebrate Victoria's Golden Jubilee. More plantings took place in 1977 and 1980 for the Queen's Silver Jubilee and the Queen Mother's eightieth birthday. May Hill, it would appear, is a symbol for many causes... 971 feet high, although hardly seeming it, its dome is unmistakable from any angle, be it in the Severn Vale or along the Cotswold edge. And John Masefield was not the last poet to be inspired by the brooding mystery of its silhouette.

*

Notwithstanding the obvious qualities of the north-west Gloucestershire countryside, why should a group of young ambitious poets come to Dymock of all places? Partly it was a question of circumstance; there was a drift from the land in the first decade of the twentieth century, which accelerated up to the Great War. There was more and more employment in the towns and less each year in the country, with the chances for an apparently better life for people used to generations of rural poverty. Rather than scratching a living from the land, there was now the possibility — more, almost a promise that had made itself through the nineteenth century — of a more attractive exciting life in an urban environment. Whatever the reality that underlay this dream, the fact was that landowners found themselves with estate workers' cottages on their hands, and fewer and fewer tenants to fill them. So the arrival of outsiders eager to pay good rental for otherwise fallow properties was clearly something to be welcomed wholeheartedly.

There was also the fact of improved rail communication with outlying rural areas, a link with the main metropolitan centres that made previously remote parts of the country increasingly accessible. The railway track had been extended from Gloucester to Ledbury, with a full passenger service from Ledbury to Over Junction opening on 27 July 1885, the ultimate conclusion of a curious set of circumstances. As early as 1873 two companies, the Ross and Ledbury Railway and the Newent Railway, received approval to build lines, one from Ledbury to Ross via Dymock, the other from Dymock to Over, west of Gloucester. The two companies could not raise the necessary funding, and three years later G.W.R. stepped in and a Ledbury to Gloucester line was built, while the Ross section was abandoned before it was begun. For the most part the railway followed the route of the old Hereford and Gloucester canal, which had been opened in March 1798, and which was now drained for the purpose. In 1892, seven years after opening, the Ross and Ledbury Railway and the Newent Railway were finally officially absorbed by G.W.R. who originally perceived the line not as the branch it later became, but as a means of linking Gloucester and Birmingham in competition with their rivals, the Midland Railway. Thus through traffic used the line until 1907, when another, more direct route was opened. Up until the First World War the Ledbury to Dymock track was double; then in 1917 one set of lines was removed, and used overseas as part of the war effort. Dymock station gained a reputation as one of the most beautiful in England, and its flower gardens enchanted generations of passengers up until its closure. Here in springtime thousands of workers imported from as far away as London would arrive to help with the daffodil harvest. At this time G.W.R. would run extra trains, so busy did the area become. Hence the affectionate name, "The Daffodil Line", which remained until 11 July 1959, when an 0-6-0 Collett 3203 engine, crewed by Fireman Jim Kavanagh and Driver Jack Folley, pulled the last passenger train between Ledbury and Gloucester. With that the Ledbury-Dymock line closed to all traffic, to be followed on 30 May 1964 by the final closure of the line between Dymock and Over Junction. An era in transport history was over here, as it was ending on so many small branch lines around Britain at the time, and cutting a link between rural and urban centres. Fifty years earlier the railway had provided that link that was partially the enabling factor in the birth and growth of the Dymock group of poets. So it was that in the years before the First World War, it would have been possible for those wishing to enjoy a country life while not severing ties with the big cities to have the best of both worlds: to live the imagined idyll of timeless rural England, while knowing that an editor or publisher was only a train ride away.

But there was another, more specific set of circumstances through which Dymock chose itself. The family of poets who came to Dymock grew organically, to a degree naturally, but also coincidentally. And once a nucleus had been formed, more were brought into that hub. It was a case of like minds attracting one another. The real, most practical answer to the question 'Why Dymock?' is to be found in the fact that Lascelles Abercrombie, a discontented quantity surveyor with a burning desire to write, had a sister who married a gentleman farmer, and came to live in a cottage on the Beauchamp estate at Much Marcle, some three miles away from Dymock, and just across the border in Herefordshire. In fact, Abercrombie had already made his commitment to literature by the time he came to the area; his first volume of poems, *Interludes and Poems* had been published in 1908, and from 1907 to 1909 he was a leading critic on the *Liverpool Daily Courier* and the *Daily Post* succeeding Dixon Scott. Born a Lancashire man at Aston-Upon-Mersey in 1881, he had received his higher education at Owen's College, Manchester, although his early academic life had been spent at Malvern College. The likelihood is that Abercrombie came for a visit to his older sister and brother-in-law, and was stirred by memories of his childhood spent in the area. Whether or not he had explored the fields and lanes of the Dymock countryside during his time at Malvern College as a boy, we do not know. The College magazine in Abercrombie's time was more a record of sporting and academic achievements — in that order — rather than a repository of personal accounts and literary or artistic contributions of the sort more familiar today. That apart, his time at the college may well hold the ultimate answer to the question 'Why Dymock?' and it may have been the memory of those days that led him back here, and indeed brought him back for visits to the area until the end of his life. During his time at Malvern, a sensitive boy responsive to landscape could not have escaped the spell of the area, and the variety of its topography. The very proximity of the Malvern Hills, their grandeur, and the contrasting intimacy of the small Dymock fields with their glory of daffodils in springtime must have made this almost a return to Eden to Lascelles Abercrombie. This combined with a growing feeling that he must throw off his present way of life and give himself up to his instinct for poetry, and in 1910 he came to live at Much Marcle with his wife Catherine. Abercrombie had already had one collection of poems published, which had attracted no less a critic than Edward Thomas, one of the most respected reviewers on the current literary scene. Thomas had written a notice of the book in the *Daily Chronicle* and had been impressed enough to comment on the new arrival to his friend Gordon Bottomley:

> It cost me two whole days...He is good there is no doubt...[he] has his own vocabulary and a wonderful variety in his blank verse...though I have written a review of the book I have not made up my mind about it except that it is the sincere work of an artist. I wonder what he is like...

Favourable attention from a critic of the calibre of Thomas must have increased Abercrombie's ambition. Thomas, born in London of Welsh parents in 1878, possessed a distinguished reputation as a critic of poetry, a man of whom Thomas Seccombe wrote: "He was the man with the Keys to the Paradise of English poetry, and probably reviewed more modern verse than any critic of his time". He could make, but he could also perhaps break a reputation. Edward Thomas was demanding in his criticism, and was not slow to perceive mediocrity. He asked much of the writers he reviewed, just as he asked much of himself. Praise therefore from Thomas was praise indeed, and Lascelles would have been encouraged to continue. From his temporary home at Much Marcle, Abercrombie published a pamphlet, dedicated to "my mother", of his poem, 'Mary and the Bramble':

> The great blue ceremony of the air
> Did a new morrow for the earth prepare;
> The silver troops of mist were almost crept
> Back to the streams where through the day they slept;
> And, high up on his tower of song, the glad
> Galloping wings of a lark already had
> A message from the sun, to give bright warning
> That he would shortly make a golden morning.

For Abercrombie that golden morning was just beginning. He was shaking himself free of the old life, a life he had lived as some sort of duty rather than in any sense a vocation. Now, back in this beloved landscape, with his sister at Much Marcle, he had a foothold on a new existence. It was now or never. On his behalf, his sister approached Lord Beauchamp, her landlord, and asked him if any of his cottages were currently available. His lordship was able to offer a number of options, among them a house in the hamlet of Ryton, a mile or so east of Dymock. The house was called 'The Gallows', a most charming half-timbered cottage — or rather a pair of linked cottages — reached by a set of steep steps from the sunken lane, and backing onto the dense wood of Ryton Firs, and in Spring surrounded by wild daffodils and primroses. It was an ideal opportunity; the house had recently been renovated for one of Beauchamp's land agents, and represented a high standard of living for the time and the place. The smaller of the two cottages, which Abercrombie called "The Study", was by far the older, black and white half-timbering with a thatched roof, pitched steeply down to below head-height, thatched, according to Abercrombie's account, with a base of two or three hundred year old rye grass, topped up occasionally with wheat straw. Here, in the principal downstairs room, Lascelles set up his writing materials, using the upstairs rooms as bedrooms for himself, Catherine and their two children. From this cottage ran a passage into the other building, built of native red sandstone with a considerable additional structure at the rear containing a kitchen, pantry and shed. Upstairs there were three more bedrooms. Spacious indeed, lacking only proper sanitation, but all freshly overhauled and ready for occupation. As it turned out, the man for whom the property had been prepared had left the area, and so at the very moment Abercrombie had expressed interest in settling back in this part of England, the perfect home had become available.

The house had gained its name as the result of a local legend revolving around a character from Dymock's indeterminate folk history. The man, "Jock of Dymock", was said to have terrorised passers-by, by rushing out at them on gusty moonlight nights with a set of antlers strapped to his head. Jock met his end when he was caught at Ryton poaching deer belonging to the king. He was hanged on the spot, and the house that was later built on the site commemorated the event in its name. This was the cottage Lord Beauchamp offered to Abercrombie, and Lascelles did not hesitate. After just a few months at Much Marcle, he and Catherine moved to Ryton. Such was the beginning of the Dymock group, and to understand the events of the subsequent thirty-six months or so of intense literary activity in the area, it is useful to build a picture of Abercrombie's personality at this time. For it was Abercrombie around whom the group grew up, and without whom little would have been achieved. According to a friend of the time, John Haines, he was a vibrant personality, with "a gusto for life in all its activities as keen as Hazlitt's". Haines was a local solicitor, about whose contribution to the Dymock circle we shall have more to say. His first impression of Abercrombie in 1911-1912 was that of a man with a genius for the presentation of an argument, a great conversationalist and a man of considerable wit and humour. He was also — which is rare in such men — a wonderful listener, radiating "fascination with all the culture of a scholar, the subtlety of a philosopher and the charm of a happy and kindly man". His reading voice was beautiful and mellifluous, and he used it almost as a musical instrument. Haines recalled that "I never doubted the excellence of his verse save when he read it, and then only because his delivery of it was so beautiful I hardly knew or cared what it meant".

That summer saw a record-breaking heat wave, with temperatures up to ninety-seven degrees. During the first week in August, so great was the heat that there was a mortality rate of 855 in London. Also in August there were strikes and riots against pay and conditions in London and Liverpool, following similar disturbances in Wales. Earlier in the year Ramsay MacDonald was elected as the new Labour Party chairman, while in November Bonar Law succeeded

Balfour as the leader of the Tories. Winston Churchill, aided by his secretary Edward Marsh, was named as the new First Lord of the Admiralty.

During April a new deal for writers was heralded with the second reading of the Copyright Bill, which provided for the application of copyright throughout an author's lifetime and for fifty years after the death of that author, so ending more than a century of plagiarism and injustice for men and women of letters. And in June came the coronation of a new king. In a seven hour ceremony at Westminster Abbey, George V was crowned "King of the United Kingdom of Great Britain and Ireland and of the British Dominions beyond the seas, Defender of the Faith, Emperor of India". The Georgian era that was to give its name to the most popular literary movement of its time had begun.

The symbols were of a stirring new world. Somehow Britain had until now not really shaken itself free of the long flowing cloak of Victoria. Now it seemed that fresh air was blowing through the country again. Abercrombie must have felt his new situation to be a metaphor. That he fell in love with his new home is evident in every line of his most famous poem, 'Ryton Firs':

> From Marcle way,
> From Dymock, Kempley, Newent, Bromeberrow,
> Redmarley, all the meadowland daffodils seem
> Running in golden tides to Ryton Firs...

> ...Then warm moist hours steal in,
> Such as can raw the year's
> First fragrance from the sap of cherry wood
> Or from the leaves of budless violets;
> And travellers in lanes
> Catch the hot tawny smell
> Reynard's damp fur left as he sneakt marauding
> Across from gap to gap:
> And in the larch woods on the highest boughs
> The long-eared owls like grey cats sitting still
> Peer down to quiz the passengers below.

> Light has killed the winter and all dark dreams.
> Now winds live all in light,
> Light has come down to earth and blossoms here,
> And we have golden minds.

2. The Literary Scene

The Edwardian Age had been peopled by poets whose abilities and styles varied hugely. Hardy and Yeats were there of course, as were Kipling, Chesterton, Noyes and Masefield. Also widely read were Robert Bridges, Laurence Binyon and Walter de la Mare. The Poet Laureate was the much ridiculed Alfred Austin, a diminutive and humourless man, whose first and most dramatic claim to fame had been his poem in praise of the Jameson raid, an ill-conceived attempt to overthrow the Boer resistance in Africa. The poem, written within days of his appointment in 1896, infuriated Victoria, and actually moved Britain closer to outright confrontation with the Boers:

> Wrong! Is it wrong? Well, may be:
> But I'm going, boys, all the same.
> Do they think me a burgher's baby,
> To be scared by a scolding name?
> They may argue, and prate, and order;
> Go, tell them to save their breath:
> Then, over the Transvaal border,
> And gallop for life or death!

Punch at once seized on the poet and poem, and produced a parody that mauled both the content and the technique:

> Say, is it song? Well — blow it!
> But I'll sing it, boys, all the same
> Because I'm the Laureate Poet,
> That's the worst of having a name!
> I must be inspired to order,
> Go, tell 'em to save their breath!

I can rhyme to 'order' with 'border',
And jingle to 'breath' with 'death'.

Jameson went to prison for fifteen months. Austin remained as
Laureate for another seventeen years, until his death in 1913. Al-
though he never achieved anything quite so tasteless again, his long
years in the post made the position a joke. The true essence of
Edwardian poetic thought was however rather different. In 1900,
Yeats wrote that "Beauty is the end and law of poetry", while for
Sturge Moore, poetry and art existed for the "evocation, develop-
ment and perpetuation of beauty". Robert Bridges saw the poet as
"the man who is possessed by the idea of beauty". In 1909 Oxford's
Professor of Poetry A.C. Bradley published his *Oxford Lectures on
Poetry* in which he stated:

> About the best poetry...there floats an atmosphere of infinite
> suggestion. The poet speaks to us of one thing, but in this one
> thing there seems to lurk the secret of all...It is a spirit. It comes
> we know not whence. It will not speak at our bidding, nor
> answer in our language. It is not our servant; it is our master.
> [pp 26-7]

There were of course exceptions to this aura of mysticism which
hung around the idea of the poetic impulse. Swinburne — a strong
influence on many — had died in 1909, as had Meredith. Hardy was
now the senior survivor of the Victorian poets. His collection of that
year, *Time's Laughingstocks*, included some of his finest work. Rooted
firmly in his place — Wessex — he spoke with a universal voice
linked to a traditional although infinitely varied technique. Here the
spirit of place, and the men and women that peopled that place, was
clear, human and moving. And anyone who thought that he was
writing his swan-song would have been forced to think again.
Hardy, approaching his seventieth birthday, still had five more
collections before him. Of this achievement, Ezra Pound was later to
say that Hardy's sheer size of output, together with its all-embracing
clarity and reality, was almost elemental in its nature, and left little
place "for the explaining critic". Hardy's monolithic figure seems to
exist independent of all trends, transcending fashion and carving its
own line through the poetry of all nineteenth and twentieth century
periods and movements. He stands somehow separate from the
battleground that was about to be fought over by the young preten-

ders in Edwardian England.

For this ground came challenges from all sides, including, from outside the post-Victorian establishment, a gauntlet thrown down by Pound himself. Edward Thomas, living near Petersfield in Hampshire, writing against the clock to maintain an existence for himself and his young family in a rented cottage called Berryfield, discovered in that same year of 1909 the work of the 24-year-old American, who had recently established himself in London, in Church Walk, Kensington. The two men met at the influential Square Club, frequented by the fashionable literati of the time, such men as Edgar Jepson, G.K. Chesterton and H.W. Nevinson. Thomas was a respected and perceptive reviewer with an as yet unguessed-at career as a poet ahead of him, and he wrote a significant notice of Pound's new book *Personae* for *The English Review*. With hindsight we may see a corner about to be turned:

> To say what this poet has not is not difficult; it will help us to define him. He has no obvious grace, no sweetness, hardly any of the superficial good qualities of modern versifiers; not the smooth regularity of the Tennysonian tradition, nor the wavering, uncertain languor of the new, though there is more in his rhythms than is apparent at first through his carelessness of ordinary effects. He has not the current melancholy or resignation or unwillingness to live; nor the kind of feeling for nature that runs to minute description and decorative metaphor. He cannot be usefully compared with any living writers... From the first to the last lines of most of his poems he holds us steadily in his own pure, grave, passionate world...

Here was Thomas the critic at his best, ending with a telling positive phrase which immediately qualifies all that has come before. In the *Daily Chronicle*, he had gone further in a review guaranteed to make traditional hackles rise:

> No remarkable melody; no golden words shot with meaning; a temperate use of images, and none far-fetched; no flattering of modern fashions in descriptions of nature; no apostrophe, no rhetoric, nothing "Celtic". It is the old miracle that cannot be defined: nothing more than a subtle entanglement of words, so that they rise out of their graves and sing.

The 29-year-old Thomas had, not for the last time, written a review that was crucial to a new poet's career. He had also seen the conception if not the birth of a new movement, or to be more precise, movements. For the reaction that was in Pound's poetry against what he was later to call the "emotional slither", "rhetorical din and luxurious riot" of the late Victorians was also the impetus that was ultimately to fire the movement that was to call itself 'Georgian'.

Thomas was to identify the same crucial quality in Thomas Hardy's *Time's Laughingstocks*: "He is not in the least afraid of colloquial prose". This was hard enough to swallow, but at least Hardy was a major name. But this was still 1909, and the revolution had not yet come. The effect of this prophetic piece of work — as Thomas's review of Pound came to be seen — was at the time dramatic in the extreme. There was a literary status quo, and this young man with his wild claims for an unknown and, what was more, American, poet had committed what seemed to many to be tantamount to a crime, as Jepson later remarked of the reaction at the Square Club:

> You could not be a poet in those days unless they discovered and made you. They would not allow it... Then E.T. fairly tore it: in a review he praised the verse of Ezra Pound! I shall never forget the meeting of the Square Club a few days after that monstrous action: the pale, shocked, contorted faces of the poet-makers... Poor Edward Thomas! He did look so hot and bothered. His protest that he had acted in good faith, that at the time of the writing of the review he had really fancied that he liked the verse of Ezra Pound, drew from his colleagues only horrid rumblings. How could he have liked the verse of a man whom none of them had discovered, much less made? Why, none of them even knew him! The thoughtlessness! The betrayal! The shattering blow to English Literature! [EJ]

Meanwhile on the other side of the Atlantic another American, a New Englander, was studying at Harvard. He had taught himself Italian by reading Dante's *Divine Comedy*, and had discovered the work of Jules Laforgue in Arthur Symons' *The Symbolist Movement in Literature*. Later Thomas Stearns Eliot was to recall: "The form in which I began to write, in 1908 or 1909, was directly drawn from the study of Laforgue together with the later Elizabethan drama". Eliot's first volume *Prufrock and other Observations* was not to appear until 1917, although several of the poems date from the Harvard years.

Notably they are 'Preludes', 'Rhapsody on a Windy Night', 'Portrait of a Lady', 'La Figlia Che Piange' and 'The Love Song of J. Alfred Prufrock', this last being written over a number of years at Harvard and in Paris. It is "poetry of place" all right. But here we are a million miles away from Sturge Moore's idealistic vision of "the artist" and Bridges' images of beauty. But then was not Rupert Brooke striving towards the same point of expression in his own way with his 'Channel Passage' sonnet?

> Do I forget you? Retchings twist and tie me,
> Old meat, good meals, brown gobbets, up I throw.
> Do I remember? Acrid return and slimy,
> The sobs and slobber of last year's woe.
> And still the sick ship rolls. 'Tis hard, I tell ye,
> To choose 'twixt love and nausea, heart and belly.

Brooke, writing to Marsh, identified that there are "common and sordid things" in which suddenly a tragic essence, "or at least the brutality of actual emotions" manifests itself. Brooke seized these, consciously if excessively, as an antidote to what he called "rosy mists of poets' experiences".

Were Brooke and Eliot touched by the same sense of rebellion? Perhaps. Were they then moving forward in a similar way? The answer to any such question must be, in the end, no. Brooke's was a subjective and, like others among the Georgians we shall consider, a rather selective realism. Whatever the differences, however attitudes varied towards the nature of change, the tide of opinion among the new writers emerging during the Edwardian age was that change of some sort was due, and was on the way. As John Middleton Murry wrote in the Summer 1911 edition of the literary journal *Rhythm*:

> ...every note of the eternal music blends in one harmony; but
> a criticism and an aestheticism fixed in the past would create
> a symphony of a single chord, which has lost its living charm,
> unappreciated, almost unheard. Until the day when the last
> note is sounded the Life of the world and the Life of art hang
> upon seeking new chords to create new harmonies.

Everywhere traditional values were under seige from the new Modernism. In music Stravinsky was writing his greatest works,

'The Firebird' (1910), 'Petrushka' (1911) and most radical of all 'The Rite of Spring' (1913). In art the great scandal of the years 1907-14 involved itself with the Cubist movement. The title, originally coined by a scornful public, described a group that had grown out of a number of influences, but particularly Cezanne's work, and his conception of painting as "a construction after nature". This is not the place for a detailed description of the complexities of the movement; suffice it to say that artists such as Picasso ('Les Demoiselles d'Avignon', 1906-07, is identified by many as the first Cubist painting), Marcel Duchamp and Jacques Villon created a movement which, although curtailed by the outbreak of the First World War, continued to be an influence in the subsequent emergence of abstract painting. One of the dichotomies of the age was that the present was being attacked by the future even while it was striving to break free of the past. In the end that was to be the fatal flaw in the Georgian movement. Brooke's "unpleasantness" might seem modernist, but his syntax harks back to an earlier time. In fact it was Brooke's misconception — indeed that of the whole movement — that the Georgians represented something of a rebellion against the Victorians. In fact it was really the same mixture, modified in a diminished form. This "new dawn" for English poetry could be seen, at least in its most ordinary moments, as the old art form bumping along the bottom. We shall consider this in more depth in the next chapter.

*

The people who were to be the components of the Dymock story were generally familiar with one another's work long before the bond of locality turned them into what history will always see as a cohesive group. Rupert Brooke and Edward Thomas had known one another for a number of years from meetings near Petersfield when Brooke was making clandestine visits to Steep to be near his Bedales love, Noel Olivier. Later at Brooke's invitation they met at Grantchester. Thomas was to review *Poems*, published in 1911, for the *Daily Chronicle*: "Copies should be bought by everyone over forty who has never been under forty. It will be a revelation. Also if they live yet a little longer they may see Mr Rupert Brooke a poet. He will not be a little one". Later still, in the Spring of 1913, Thomas was one of the judges — the others being T.E. Hulme, Harold Monro, Henry Newbolt, Edward Marsh and Ernest Rhys — who awarded Brooke first prize in a competition to find the best poem published during the previous year in Monro's *Poetry Review*. The lines on Grantchester won the prize, and Brooke was doubly pleased, with the cheque for £30, but more "in defeating Sturge Moore and James Stephens and Gibson and Abercrombie and several others who are really better than I...".

Thomas, in his role as a respected critic of poetry, although not yet of course a poet himself, held an ambivalent position in the minds of many writers of the time. His views were sought after, and his perception was deeply valued. On the other hand he could be devastating in his honesty; he spoke for what he believed in, and spoke out when he felt cause. When Abercrombie's *Interludes and Poems* was published in 1908, Thomas commented in a February edition of the *Daily Chronicle*: "He has that most modern of modern qualities, the feeling for what is primitive...". Two months later in the same paper he wrote of Gibson, who had published two volumes — *The Stonefolds* and *On the Threshold* — in 1907, in far from complimentary terms, complaining that "he has merely been embellishing what would have been far more effective as pieces of rough prose... The verse has added nothing except unreality, not even brevity". Interestingly, the relationship between prose and poetry was to be of prime importance in the development of Thomas's own art. In the meantime he found Gibson to be "essentially a minor poet in the bad sense, for he is continually treating subjects poetically, writing about things instead of creating them". Not everyone at the time would have agreed with Thomas; Gibson was a rising and shining star, and this was strong criticism in every sense. But by all accounts the poets remained friends, if not close ones.

Edward Marsh, who was to be so much a crucial part in the whole Georgian story as well as that of the Dymock group, was born in Guilford Street, Bloomsbury on 18 November 1872. He is remembered particularly for his publication of the Georgian anthologies, and for his patronage of Rupert Brooke, but his influence was wide and diverse. Marsh was a bachelor Civil Servant, during the crucial years prior to the First World War, and Secretary to Winston Churchill at the Admiralty. He was also an artistic amateur in the true sense of that word, a man of wide culture and taste, whose London home became the centre of a circle of wit, sparkling conversation and 'civilised' appreciation of the finer things in life. He was deeply impressed by the new young poets of the time, and in particular Rupert Brooke, just down from Cambridge at the time of their first meeting. Without Marsh, the term 'Georgian' would never have existed.

The focus of any debate about Georgian Realism and Modernist Realism must be a definition of the term itself. For Georgian Realism had little to do with close study of social reality. Office workers and bank clerks were not the stuff of which typically it was made; rather it saw itself as encapsulating a rugged ideal, embodied for instance in the life of the sailor, the hunter or, significantly, the soldier. It also set out consciously to shock. The desire for the disagreeable, deliberately invoked in Brooke's sonnet, was also to reach its height, and some would say its true purpose, in the First World War. It was also a realism that sought to express the elemental in human feeling, as found in an idealized view of the poor as the fount of a pure raw truth, a reaction against intellectual clutter. The Georgians looked to a simpler set of values than that which they saw growing up around them, the world that was to be claimed by the Modernists. Such romanticism is clearly represented by the work of Wilfrid Wilson Gibson, born in Battle Hill Terrace, Hexham, Northumberland in October 1878. In later years he was remembered and anthologised for a few poems such as 'Flannan Isle' and 'The Ice Cart', but his output was vast, and in his time, he was widely read.

Gibson was the son of a local chemist, and much of his education came from private tuition under his elder sister. From his earliest days he had set his sights on poetry as a career and a life. His first volume *The Golden Helm* was published in 1902 when he was twenty-four. This was quickly followed by another, equally 'bardic' title, *Urlyn the Harper*. Then in 1907 came a volume that for the first time embodied the spirit of Gibson's 'new' subject matter and content, *Stonefolds*, showing a more colloquial approach in a collection of dramatic scenes involving shepherds and other people of the fells. In 1910, the style was consolidated in *Daily Bread*, in which Gibson turned his attention to the urban poor, and the inhabitants of the mining communities he saw around him. He was to write of "the heartbreak in the heart of things", and certainly he was to capture a large audience with his images of everyday unsung tragedies:

> What fettle mate? To me he said
> As he went by
> With lifted head
> And laughing eye

Where, black against the dawning red
The pit heaps cut the sky.
What fettle mate?

What fettle mate? to him I said
As he went by
With shrouded head
And darkened eye,
Borne homeward by his marrers, dead,
Beneath the noonday sky —
What fettle, mate?

This poem — 'The Greeting' — was to appear in the second edition of *New Numbers*, the Dymock-based journal produced by Gibson and Abercrombie in 1914. Although his home landscape was a major source of his early inspiration, by 1912 he was feeling the need to move amongst other writers, to share experience and be a part of something bigger in literary terms than Hexham was able to offer. So he made for London, thereafter only returning to his native soil for short visits. It was a propitious year to undertake such an adventure, and a number of circumstances helped Gibson gain a foothold on the London literary scene. Middleton Murry and Katherine Mansfield found him lodgings, and introduced him to Edward Marsh, who helped Gibson anonymously by paying his salary as an assistant editor of *Rhythm*, destined at the time to have barely a year to survive, but in the meantime to provide him with income at a critical period. By simply being where he was Gibson was thrown into a bewildering world of literary celebrities. On one evening alone, he found himself at a discussion evening with T.E. Hulme, Ezra Pound, Murry and Marsh, as well as new names from the world of art including Nevinson, Gaudier-Brzeska and Wadsworth. For this shy, deeply impressionable man, a writer who was all his life to be a collector of reminiscences, such evenings must have been memorable. And he was to be a man in the right place at the right time as far as the immediate literary history of England was concerned. It was the birth-year of Harold Monro's Poetry Bookshop, where Gibson was to meet his wife Geraldine. It was also the year of the official conception, under Edward Marsh, of what was to be known as the 'Georgian' era.

*

Elsewhere in Britain threads were being woven that would add further to the developing web of poetry and poets. In 1904 Barry Jackson, a 25-year-old man with dreams of his own theatre company in Birmingham, was introduced to a clerk from the local branch of the Northern Assurance Company. This was John Drinkwater, a writer of lyric poetry and eager for artistic glory. Jackson's company, initially known as 'The Pilgrim Players', included Drinkwater as secretary, later manager, and as actor (under the name 'John Darnley'). Later Drinkwater was to serve Birmingham with many of his own plays, including, after the official foundation of the famous Birmingham Repertory Theatre in 1913, *Ser Taldo's Bride* (written with Jackson), *Rebellion*, *The God of Quiet* and notably *Abraham Lincoln*. Verse drama was to be an important part of the age, and something passionately advocated by Drinkwater and his fellow dramatists Gordon Bottomley and Abercrombie. This great theatre was in its early stages of construction at precisely the time the 'Georgian' poets were giving themselves a name. In the meantime Drinkwater, born in Essex in 1882 and so four years younger than Gibson, continued writing his verse, which even attracted interest from W.B. Yeats. In his 1912 volume *Poems of Love and Earth* he nailed his colours to a mast that was guaranteed to make him a founder-Georgian:

> My words are here of immemorial things,
> The labouring earth, the swift unwearied wings
> Of Love that ever circle earth about,
> Pity for stricken men and pride that they
> Yet look with eyes heroic on the day,
> Creators in the void and lords of doubt...

*

There was everywhere a new artistic scent in the air. Wherever one looked, however one interpreted it, the feeling was that the world was young again and ready for the taking. In May 1912 the premiere of Nijinsky's new ballet 'L'Après Midi d'un Faune', to music by Debussy, had created a scandal and a sensation in Paris, caused largely by the last moments of the ballet, in which Nijinsky's choreography was so erotic as to be declared by some critics as bestial. In the first edition of Harold Monro's *Poetry Review* in 1912 Lascelles Abercrombie wrote:

33

> The present is a time fermenting with tremendous change; the most tremendous of all changes, a change in the idealistic interpretation of the universe... To any man with brain and spirit active and alert in him, the present is a time wherein the world, and the destiny of man in the world, are ideas different from anything that has ever been before. If there is any resemblance at all...the present resembles more the time of the pre-Socratic Greek philosophers...than any other time. These disturbing periods, indeed, seem to recur regularly, in vast pulsations, through man's history. They are exciting but fearfully exacting times for the poet.

It was natural that the new opportunities offered by such times would be seized on in different ways. To put it another way, the battle in pre-war literature was between not left and right, but left and centre. (The right wing in English poetry during 1912 hardly existed at all.) For the rest, the Centrists, including Gibson, Abercrombie, Brooke et al, were to be pitched against the Leftists, among them Pound and Wyndham Lewis. It is interesting to note here that the latter two are normally remembered today for their right-wing phases; in the Georgian era all that lay in the future.

On the other side of the Atlantic, the struggling Robert Frost was tossing a coin to decide the future of his family of a wife and four children. Time was running out for him. He was thirty-eight. If he was to be a poet, it must be now. His wife Elinor had expressed a desire that they should go to England and "live under thatch". In Frost's mind, it was either England or Vancouver, but as he later said: "The coin chose England". From Boston, in the summer of 1912, the Frosts came across to Glasgow on a steamer called the *SS Parisian*. The ship sailed shortly before 5.00 a.m. on 24 August. She had been delayed for a few hours because some freight had not arrived on time; in the end she sailed with a full complement of passengers, 46,665 bushels of wheat and 211 barrels of apples. Elinor Frost's letter home describes the adventure in almost breathless excitement:

> ...Two weeks from the day of our decision, we were on our way out of Boston Harbour. We stored our furniture, and brought only bedclothes, two floor rugs, books, and some pictures. [SLRF p.53]

It would seem that the family experienced seasickness, although the younger members appear to have escaped. The Frosts must have been conscious, as must have been all sea-going passengers, that only a few months earlier in April 1912 the 'unsinkable' White Star liner *Titanic*, on her maiden voyage from Southampton to New York, had gone down after striking an iceberg, with the loss of more than 1,500 lives. There is little hint of how trying the journey must have been otherwise, although the exhilaration of the adventure seems to have made it more bearable:

> We landed at Glasgow in the morning, and travelled all day across Scotland and England, arriving at London about seven o'clock. [SLRF p.53]

It was 3 September. At the railway station they telephoned the Premier Hotel in Russell Square, London to book rooms, then set off at once for the capital by train, travelling for several hours and eventually arriving at 7.00 p.m. at the end of what must have been an exhausting day. The Premier was hardly a luxury hotel, although it was annexed to the more impressive Imperial Hotel. When Frost returned to England in 1928 he stayed in Russell Square again, although this time at the Imperial. Later, in 1963, the old Premier was demolished and the President Hotel erected on the site. Here at the Premier they stayed for their first ten days in England, while Robert hunted for a house to rent. In the meantime the family indulged in a mixture of emotions, "feeling greatly excited...at being all alone, without a single friend, in the biggest city in the world". Elinor — normally a subdued and delicate spirit — was at once in love with London:

> ...Nearly every evening Mr Frost and I went to the theatre. London is splendid. The absence of elevated railways and trolley cars make it a much more beautiful city than New York... [SLRF p.53]

Among the evenings at the theatre enjoyed by Mr & Mrs Frost was one on their very first night, when they saw *Fanny's First Play* by Bernard Shaw. Life must have seemed very good, although reality stepped in sharply when Frost tried to find the "thatch" under which to live. It was not a search he was equipped for, but, under helpful guidance, he found himself some twenty miles from London, in the Buckinghamshire town of Beaconsfield, where he found a property in Reynolds Road called 'The Bungalow'. The area had become something of a 'new village', having grown up around G.W.R.'s station when the line was established in 1906 to the north of the existing town. The house was quite new, one of three that had been built in 1910. Whether or not the name of the estate agent, A.C. Frost, had anything to do with the decision, we can but speculate. In any event, the family settled on it and moved in on 13 September 1912; for Elinor it had "a large grassy space in front, a pretty garden behind, with pear trees, strawberry beds and lots of flowers". It was also covered in vines. For Robert it would suffice for the time being that they were "within a mile or two of where Milton finished *Paradise Lost* on the one hand and a mile or two from where Gray lies buried on the other and within as many rods as furlongs of the house where Chesterton tries truth to see if it won't prove as true upside down as it does right side up...". At this time Reynolds Road was still edged by countryside, with a farm — Seeley's Farm on its north side. Accommodation must have been cramped for two adults and four children, but it served its purpose.

Eighteen months after the Reynolds Road time Frost's short months in Gloucestershire became significant for English poetry, and for himself as a poet and a man. But the Beaconsfield time gave him and his family some sort of initial base, albeit later not easily identifiable, since Frost himself, in a visit in 1957, could not readily recognise the house in which he and his family had first established a home in England. In the early 1990's 'The Bungalow' ceased to exist.

Back in the United States, on 5 November, Woodrow Wilson, Governor of New Jersey, won the presidential election, the first Democrat to be elected since Grover Cleveland in 1892. Not that it was a resounding victory; Wilson won only forty-two percent of the vote, beating the Progressive candidate Theodore Roosevelt and the incumbent President Taft, who won only two States. A surprisingly high vote went to Socialist candidate Eugene Debs, and some three quarters of the votes went to candidates calling for change of one sort or another.

And an American Indian, Jim Thorpe, was the hero of the fifth Olympiad of modern times, held in Stockholm. Thorpe not only won the pentathlon, but also won the decathlon by a remarkable 680 points. A few months later Thorpe was stripped of both titles when he admitted that he had been paid twenty-five dollars a week to play minor league baseball in North Carolina in 1909 and 1910. On the

English arts scene, the big show from America was 'Hello Ragtime!', written by Irving Berlin. The show had two hit numbers: 'Everybody's Doing It', and 'Alexander's Ragtime Band', sung in a new style known as 'Coon Shouting'. It was a great year for the Music Hall, and on 2 July, the Palace Theatre London was decorated with three million roses for the Royal Command Performance. The King and Queen saw Harry Tate, Little Tich and Vesta Tilley, together with George Robey and Harry Lauder, although Marie Lloyd did not appear due to a professional dispute. Anna Pavlova danced 'The Dying Swan'. In the world of the visual arts, the radical continued to attack the orthodox; London saw its first Italian futurist exhibition in which Boccioni, Russolo and Balla among others sought to interpret motion and noise in visual terms.

On the domestic front, one of the year's most notable paintings was 'Ennui' by Walter Sickert. These were the events which the Frosts would have encountered as they arrived in England in the latter half of 1912. What might have attracted less attention was an event which occurred in July of that year, when Britain decided to withdraw her battleships from the Mediterranean, to place them on patrol in the North Sea in response to a continuing German naval build-up. Winston Churchill, First Lord of the Admiralty, asked the Commons to agree an expanded naval budget, raising the sum to be spent on men and ships for the year to a record £45 million.

3. Georgian Poetry

As soon as the Abercrombies set up home at 'The Gallows' in Ryton, visits from fellow writers began. Robert Trevelyan was among the first, and, from Birmingham, John Drinkwater. In 1956 Catherine Abercrombie recalled the encounter in a radio broadcast, later published in *The Listener*, and gives us an amusing and affectionate picture of Drinkwater as poetry reader:

> I remember well [his] first arrival, very shy but very determined, and how he read some of his poems to us straight away, and how I wished he would not, as he turned himself into a fashionable parson, voice and all, and eyes to the ceiling, to do it. [TL 15 November 1956 p.793]

Meanwhile, away in London on 17 September 1912, Rupert Brooke arrived at Gray's Inn to spend a week with Edward Marsh. The man who was to become an icon for heroic youth in time of war, almost literally and almost consciously a sacrifice of youth to death in the public imagination, seems to have impressed virtually everyone he ever met with a vibrancy of physique and personality that was clearly charismatic. He was twenty-five at this first meeting, having been born in 1887, the son of a teacher at Rugby, where he was subsequently educated. He had graduated from King's College, Cambridge three years earlier in 1909. He had travelled in Europe, but had begun writing poetry while still at Rugby, and his first collection, *Poems*, had appeared in 1911. Marsh, who enjoyed cultivating relationships with all the literary lights of the time, had already perceived this golden young man as a potential star in his firmament.

As soon as Brooke arrived in the evening, he found Marsh anxious to take him out again; he had been dining with George Mallory and

Duncan Grant, and had heard that there was a major timber fire at King's Cross. Marsh wanted to see it, and the two men set out, en route picking up Wilfrid Gibson, recently arrived from Hexham. Brooke and Gibson had not previously met, but it seems they immediately made an impression on one another, setting off what almost was to amount to adulation in the latter. Gibson, ever one to turn reminiscence into verse, recalled the meeting and the fire in his elegy, 'Rupert Brooke':

> Your face was lifted to the golden sky
> Ablaze beyond the black roofs of the square
> As flame leapt, flourishing in air
> Its tumult of red stars exultantly
> To the cold constellations dim and high;
> And, as we neared, the roaring ruddy flare
> Kindled to gold your throat and brow and hair
> Until you burned, a flame of ecstasy...

After the fire, the three went back to Marsh's house, and talked into the small hours. Thus began the great friendship between Brooke and Gibson ("Wibson" as Brooke was to affectionately nickname him). Gibson was ultimately to become one of Brooke's beneficiaries, together with Marsh and Walter de la Mare. Two days later, as Marsh and Brooke sat talking alone in Edward Marsh's Gray's Inn rooms, Brooke, frustrated by the current literary scene, proposed the writing of a fictional contents page as a parody of the poor state of English verse. He would then write pastiches under the pseudonyms and publish the book. When the work had been lauded by the critics, he would expose the sham in *The Times*, as a jolt to the complacency of the present literary scene. It was lightly said, but the remark carried a frustration as to the state of things which was shared by both men. Marsh pursued the idea rather more seriously; there was a perceivable, although varied groundswell of real poets, he felt, waiting to be brought together, who by united forces, would demonstrate that there was real life in English poetry yet. Much of the impetus for this movement was to do with use of language: a shifting away from the grandiose towards everyday expression. In that sense it could be perceived as a twentieth century equivalent of the publishing in 1798 by Wordsworth and Coleridge of the *Lyrical Ballads*, a parallel that was to become more apposite in due course.

The renaissance had in fact already begun; Masefield had had a huge success with 'The Everlasting Mercy' in 1911, a poem in which the word "bloody" rather shockingly appeared. W.W. Gibson was writing poems about the everyday people he saw around him in Northumberland and there were other comparable writers, such as Ralph Hodgson and Brooke himself. With them came a chance to escape from poetic 'prettiness' and to create a new living tradition. In 1914 Lascelles Abercrombie was to articulate this in a paper for the English Association, entitled *Poetry and Contemporary Speech*:

> ...There is not only convenience but real and positive value for poetry in the use of forms like don't and won't:... Don't is not simply a contraction of do not; it is somehow another and slightly different form of verbal life.

True to his word, the day after his discussion with Brooke, Marsh set up a meeting over a meal to discuss the new concepts. It was a significant gathering, with Gibson, John Drinkwater, Harold Monro and his assistant editor at *Poetry Review*, Arundel del Re, all present. As we have seen, Brooke and Gibson had only just met three days earlier, and it was also Drinkwater's first meeting with Brooke. In 1917 he recalled the occasion:

> There were then but a few moments in which Brooke and I could talk together, and all that I can remember is an impression of an extraordinarily alert intelligence, finely equipped with both wit and penetrative power, and resolutely declining to use either for any superficial effect. I suppose no one of his years can ever have had in greater measure the gifts that can be used to make easily swayed admiration gape, or greater temptations so to employ his qualities: and I am sure that no man has ever been more wholly indifferent to any such conquests. Humour he had in abundance, but of witty insincerity no trace. Never was a personality more finely balanced. It is this that I remember of him at that first meeting... [PP p.189]

Set against that, we should remember that in terms of success and actual tangible achievement, Brooke was at this time very much the junior partner. Gibson was established, Drinkwater also, Monro and Marsh were important and influential; it might be said that Brooke had a lot to gain by being on his best behaviour. Be that as it may, on that day the Georgian Poetry movement was born, although the title pleased no one but Marsh very much; Brooke felt it smacked of conservatism. At least, Marsh argued, it placed them firmly in the new era brought about by a new king and, more importantly, it separated them clearly from the term 'Victorian'. Monro had recently acquired premises for a Poetry Bookshop at 35 Devonshire Street, not far from Marsh's home, and this, it was agreed, would be the publishing headquarters, with Gray's Inn as an editorial base. Harold Monro had been born in Brussels in 1879, and educated at Radley and at Cambridge. A poet himself, he was responsible for launching *The Poetry Review*. The Poetry Bookshop became in time far more than what its name implies; it grew to be a meeting place, some would say even a sanctuary for writers at all stages of their careers. Among subsequent publishing ventures were Charlotte Mew's poems, and from 1919-25 *The Monthly Chapbook* which was founded and edited by Monro. In 1933 his own *Collected Poems* received a critical note from T.S. Eliot. Strong friendships were born on that first Georgian meeting. Brooke wrote to Frances Cornford:

> I've been meeting a lot of poets in London. They were so nice: very simple, and very goodhearted. I felt I'd like, almost, to live with them always (and protect them). — But London won't do. [RB/GK p.402]

If all appears as if in an idealistic haze, it was not quite so. During the late summer of 1912 Robert Frost, newly arrived in Britain, soon became aware that the literary scene on this side of the Atlantic was fragmenting into factions. Marsh and his Georgians were clearly a force to be reckoned with, but there was also the young Cambridge graduate, Thomas Ernest Hulme, with his philosophical interest in theories of art. Hulme had linked with the poet F.S. Flint, whose first volume of poems *In the Net of the Stars* was published in 1909. Imagery and analogy in poetry formed the driving force behind Hulme's thinking, and it was a doctrine that had also influenced the Idaho poet Ezra Pound, then living in London. Pound was making a name for himself among writers and critics. Brooke spoke for him regarding a place in *Georgian Poetry*, and Yeats also championed his work.

A few days after the first meeting at Gray's Inn, Marsh discussed the idea of an anthology of the new poetry with John Middleton Murry and Katherine Mansfield, then approached Housman, Pound and Abercrombie. All these were possible contributors. He was also keen to include E.B. Sargant's poem 'The Cuckoo Wood' from the *Casket Songs* collection. He planned to contact Masefield, Gordon Bottomley and James Stephens, and he wrote to Walter de la Mare:

> Of course I MUST have you, if I can possibly persuade you to let me have a few things out of 'The Listeners' — that poem itself and 'Arabia', and two or three others. Do you think you could? [EM/CH p.191]

A letter to W.H. Davies brought an acceptance but on his own terms; he did not approve of Marsh's selection of his work, and proposed his 'The Kingfisher'. Pound did not feel able to release Marsh's chosen poems, but suggested his collection *Canzoni*, which Marsh rejected. By the time the second Georgian Anthology was published, Marsh's principles had been fixed against writers other than British and thus Pound and Frost were never included. Bottomley, very ill, felt unable to contribute for health reasons. D.H. Lawrence accepted, as did Chesterton, although he was later to fall by the wayside. Masefield's reaction was sceptical, as was Sturge Moore's. But James Elroy Flecker wrote that he was "very glad to appear in the company of my old friend Rupert Brooke". And there were poems by Robert Calverley Trevelyan and Harold Monro. In his 'Prefatory Note', under the anonymity of the initials 'E.M.', Marsh wrote:

> This volume is issued in the belief that English poetry is now once again putting on a new strength and beauty.

Marsh had perceived that few readers have the time or enthusiasm to study poetry assiduously, and therefore to realise that "we are at the beginning of another 'Georgian Period' which may take rank in due time with the several great poetic ages of the past". He went on:

> It has no pretension to cover the field. Every reader will notice the absence of poets whose work would be a necessary ornament of any anthology not limited by a definite aim. Two years ago some of the writers represented had published nothing; and only a very few of the others were known except to the eagerest "watchers of the skies". Those few are here because within the chosen period their work seemed to have

gained some accession of power.

That was the extent of the manifesto, and as such it surely contained little with which to argue, acknowledging as it did that here was an idiosyncratic collection which consciously adopted a stance in order to make a statement. Nevertheless there was in the Georgian temper a desire that bound many of them together, that of doing for modern verse what Wordsworth had sought to do in the *Lyrical Ballads*. A.C. Bradley had said of Wordsworth that "what he showed was what he saw". Later Abercrombie was to say that Wordsworth desired to recreate the real language of men "in a state of vivid sensation". Wordsworth at his most challenging would declare "that poetry was only the language of prose in metre". The first edition, *Georgian Poetry 1911-1912* appeared in December 1912. Abercrombie's dramatic poem 'The Sale of Saint Thomas' opened the volume; this was the long poem Abercrombie had published in 1911 shortly after arriving at Ryton, dedicating it then to "Arthur Ransome, my friend". At that publication, the author had included the following epigraph:

> The Tradition.
> When, for the gospelling of the world, the Apostles sorted the
> countries among themselves, the lot of India fell to Thomas.
> After some hesitations, he obeyed the lot, being shamed
> thereto by his Master, as is here set forth.

This statement was omitted from the Georgian volume, whether in error or deliberately is uncertain. Nevertheless, although its absence may perhaps confuse certain readers, it is arguable that its presence would have done little to rescue the poem from the dated song of its syntax:

> To India! Yea, here I may take ship;
> From here the courses go over the seas,
> Along which the intent prows wonderfully
> Nose like lean hounds, and track their journeys out,
> Making for harbours as some sleuth was laid
> For them to follow on their shifting road.
> Again I front my appointed ministry...

Rupert Brooke was represented by 'The Old Vicarage, Grantchester',

'Dust', 'The Fish', 'Town and Country', and 'Dining-room Tea':

> ...The laughter played
> Unbroken round me; and the jest
> Flashed on. And we that knew the best
> Down wonderful hours grew happier yet.
> I sang at heart, and talked, and ate,
> And lived from laugh to laugh, I too,
> When you were there, and you, and you.

Drinkwater's 'The Fires of God' was present, taken from his current volume of 1912, *Poems of Love and Earth*:

> And the ancient might
> Of the binding bars
> Waned as I woke to a new desire
> For the choice song
> Of exultant, strong
> Earth-passionate men with souls of fire.

Wilfrid Gibson's three poems included two from his volume *Fires*, the book that introduced 'Flannan Isle' to the world. These were 'The Hare' and 'Devil's Edge'. The third poem was 'Geraniums', a poem which contrasts the bright beauty of the flower with the squalid life of the flower-seller:

> So, blazing gaily red
> Against the luminous deeps
> Of starless London night,
> They burn for my delight:
> While somewhere, snug in bed,
> A worn old woman sleeps.

Among the first responses to the book was a letter to Marsh from Maurice Hewlett. In it he praised Brooke ("[He] is a poet. I have no doubt about him") and Gibson ("I always like Gibson") but his pleasure in the anthology as a whole was qualified:

> The total impression I have is that your men are interested in strength rather than Beauty, have lost a good deal of sensation, and by reason of that make an imperfect fusion of their passionate natures. I believe that the fired sense and the fired mind have to burn together to produce great imagination.

Abercrombie and Drinkwater in particular fail in this. They seem to make poetry entirely by ratiocination... [EM/CH p.205]

In particular Hewlett attacked Abercrombie's work, claiming him to have "read Bridges on Milton not wisely. It runs too thin". Marsh sent the letter on to Brooke with the message: "I agree with nearly all of it except about Lascelles". What subsequent critics complained of — and they were many — was that the Georgians did not allow for the sweeping changes that in fact overtook the concept of their creation. That view, aimed at later editions of the Georgian anthologies, in which the standard of much of the work was undeniably poorer, should not be associated with the first book, which was a huge success. Modernism was also abroad, but for a time the two existed side by side, clearly demonstrating the remarkable and exciting melting pot that was represented by the writing of the era. As the latter-day Georgian, Wallace Nichols wrote:

> The Georgians...tended to put forth their own leaves on the old boughs of tradition while Eliot led a complete change in poetics, one more rhythmical than metrical. No greater literary contrast could be afforded than a comparison between the form of *The Waste Land* and that of Alfred Noyes's *The Torchbearers*, the work roughly of the same decade and showing the definite split in verse practice already beginning to be operative. [PR Summer 1966 p.99]

Just over twenty years after Marsh's pioneering publication, Alida Monro, editing a successor to *Georgian Poetry* from the Poetry Bookshop entitled *Recent Poetry 1923-1933*, was to write with the benefit of hindsight:

> Before the first volume of E.M.'s [Edward Marsh] series was published...Ezra Pound was actively engaged in ploughing the furrows for the new crop of poetry. Between the issue of the first and second volumes he launched his collections *Des Imagistes* and *Catholic Anthology*. Both of these contained work by poets who have since fully justified his foresight in assembling it for the attention of those ready to be interested.
>
> E.M. was, quite rightly, anxious to show that there were a number of poets in this century whose work was equal to that produced in the last, and who differed more in kind than in

> degree from their Edwardian predecessors. But his ear was
> attuned to the glories of the past rather than to the poten-
> tialities of the future. Consequently, anyone who had never
> seen *Georgian Poetry* until this moment would, on studying
> the five volumes, be unaware of the very great change — apart
> from such new subjects and changes of form as were necessi-
> tated by the war — which had overtaken English poetry since
> the accession of King George. He would be unaware of the
> existence of Mr Pound's anthologies mentioned above, and of
> *The Chapbook, Coterie, Wheels, The Owl*, to mention but a few
> of the publications of the years 1911-1922 in which the new
> poetry could be found. [RP p.v-vi]

In the meantime however, it seemed that the field was clear for
Marsh's anthology, and the book's achievements were remarkable.
A year after publication the book had entered its ninth edition, and
Arundel del Re was to come to the opinion that had it not been for
Marsh and the Georgians, "poetry would have scarcely been able
either to regain its rightful public position among the arts, or to
preserve it through the war crisis and afterwards". There were many
other Georgian Poetry volumes to come, but the first book went on
selling up to the Second World War, by which time it had sold 15,000
copies, while *Georgian Poetry II* had sold 19,000 copies, very high
sales next to all but a few of today's figures. The contributors
themselves were delighted, not least by the fact that they actually
received financial remuneration. James Stephens commented with
amazement that here was an anthology that had not only gone
through many editions, but had actually succeeded "in paying its
contributors! [This] does seem like a forecast of an overdue mille-
nium". John Drinkwater wrote to Marsh: "I congratulate you most
warmly on the splendid success... We are all your grateful debtors.
Your venture has put a good livery once again on patronage". W.H.
Davies was also delighted, saying the the book's success had been
"far beyond my reckoning". D.H. Lawrence in Italy thanked Marsh
for his royalties with equal pleasure: "That *Georgian Poetry* book is a
veritable Aladdin's lamp. I little thought my 'Snapdragon' would go
on blooming and seeding in this prolific fashion. So many thanks for
the cheque for four pounds, and long life to G.P.".

Indeed long life was assured, and Lawrence, for many perhaps the
most surprising name to be found in a Georgian anthology, made an
appearance in all but one of the five volumes of the anthology

between 1911 and 1922. He was the only one of all the thirty-six poets included in the series who could possibly be called modernist, but there he remained. For the rest, Marsh's books, looked back on as if they were some kind of radical experiment, were really nothing of the kind. In the Georgian Anthologies, he simply proved what he had set out to do: that there was a popular audience prepared to buy and read poetry, that recent writing had lost touch with its audience, and was of little interest to any but scholars, and that the average potential reader, like himself, was more interested in short "human interest" lyrical poems than complex syntax and deep theories of literature and art. Marsh believed his standards and tastes were reasonably representative of a well educated middle class, and used that standard as his yardstick. To reach this audience, he had to make sure his 'product' was packaged in a way that would underline its purpose. And at this, Marsh was a genius. Often by shifting an emphasis slightly, he had the ability of widening the appeal of a poem or a poet out of all recognition. It is arguable that a poem called 'The Sentimental Exile' (Brooke's original title) would never have achieved the fame it did as 'The Old Vicarage, Grantchester' (changed at Marsh's suggestion).

It may have been in the way the verse was marketed as much as the content of the verse itself, but for whatever reason, the anthologies fulfilled their aims; Edward Marsh got people reading poetry again. Latterly the Modernists turned against the Georgians, became more esoteric in their work, and lost the mass audience. It is not the place of this book to explore the rights and wrongs of this, but it is important for a modern reader to be aware that the movement was, for want of a better word, a popular one. Seldom since the Georgian era has a non-literary audience read poetry in such significant quantity. It was not necessary to ask the audience to seek out this poetry; the anthology provided a pre-packed, ready-made source, easy to dip into at will, with no need to indulge in literary research. The finding and choosing had been done for the audience, who could feel that they were being provided with some knowledge of the cutting edge of modern poetry.

Of course they were not. But combined with presentation was content, and that too was crucial, and the time had a great deal to do with it. There was even without hindsight, a sense of change, as rural life continued to give way to urban migration. Then the war fuelled the special 'Englishness' that was so much a part of the Georgian ethic. It was, this poetry, very much a celebration of England in an idealised sense. The world that the man fighting in France would look back to would be that of thatch and country lanes and rural crafts and stable values that seemed to have stretched back through all time. Writers born in Hardy's generation lived in a world that recalled the unchanging landscape of England at the time of Wellington and before, while living to experience powered flight, radio, recording, urban slums and a greatly increased efficiency in the development of weapons of death and destruction. It was hardly surprising that with an uninviting century stretching bleakly into the invisible distance, the past should offer security.

The later criticisms of the Georgians are largely quite valid; flaccid technique, sentimentality, mawkishness, banality of themes and expression, self-consciously 'rural' and too often a lacking of intellect and imagination. Set against this must be the danger of generalisation; there were good Georgians, just as there were bad Modernists. There were poets who, because of their time, have become called Georgians, whose work transcend all these criticisms. Thus Eliot's 1917 statement in the *Times Literary Supplement* that "the Georgians caress everything they touch" is rather too general to be acceptable as a criticism of what was, after all, an extremely diverse, numerous and various group of poets. Edmund Blunden was to write perceptively about Ivor Gurney, and in doing so, to say as much about the Georgian movement as he was about the poet in question, when he said: "Whatever was attractive and poetically moving to the generation of writers called Georgians was so to him also, and he was content to be of that generation; but neither easy sentiment nor an indifferent 'eye on the object' can be imputed to him, nor yet languor nor studied homeliness of expression". The same could be said of a number of other writers, Edward Thomas being also notable in this respect. Edward Thomas never appeared in a Georgian anthology, and it would be hard to claim that his reputation would have been enhanced had he done so. Good poets are outside movements, and bad poets will not finally be saved by their inclusion in them. This then was the time and place of Georgian writing, in the context of which the Dymock group had its life, almost a microcosm of the larger movement in its reasons, tensions and ultimate demise.

4. Coming Together

Now we come back to the Dymock story. On 8 January 1913 the spiritual and practical home of the Georgian movement, Harold Monro's Poetry Bookshop, was opened officially, and less than a week after the opening, Edward Thomas reviewed its exciting new product *Georgian Poetry 1911-1912* in the following encouraging terms:

> It shows much beauty, strength, and mystery, and some magic, much aspiration, less defiance, no revolt — and it brings out with great cleverness many sides of the modern love of the simple and primitive, as seen in children, peasants, savages, early men, animals and nature in general. [DC 14 January 1913 quoted in EM/CH p.682]

The shop had been attracting poets even before the official date of its opening celebration. At this the Poetry Bookshop had been crammed with three hundred people, including many of the poets whose careers were bound up with its success. Among them — though it would appear that Thomas did not meet him — was Robert Frost, still imperfectly settled in The Bungalow in Reynolds Road, Beaconsfield. Frost was at this time looking forward to the publication less than three months later of his collection *A Boy's Will*, taking its title from a passage in Longfellow's 'My Lost Youth':

> A boy's will is the wind's will
> And the thoughts of youth are long, long thoughts.

It was not Thomas that Frost met at the Poetry Bookshop, but Frank S. Flint — later to review *A Boy's Will* sympathetically — who urged him to make the aquaintance of Ezra Pound. Eventually Pound and

Frost did meet, at the former's home in the little lane, narrow then as now, called Church Walk, Kensington. It was to be the autumn before the ultimately more momentous meeting between Frost and Thomas took place. Nevertheless the meeting with Pound meant a lot to Frost, who later recalled how he was refreshed by Pound's open-minded approach to the new and good in literature. He was, as Robert remembered, "the first poet I ever sat down with to talk about poetry"; Frost was at first put out by Pound's visiting card, although he kept it for the rest of his life: "Ezra Pound, at home — sometimes".

When the new collection, a crucial volume for Frost, appeared in April, Pound seized a copy in David Nutt's office, and took it (and its author) back to Church Walk and sat reading intently. Frost, who had not even had a chance to look at the book himself, was told "Find yourself something to read". After some time Pound glanced up at Frost and said "I hope you don't mind my liking it?" Frost was non-plussed, saying "Oh, go ahead and like it," but Pound declared that he was going to review it, telling the other American to "run along home", which Frost did, still without having had more than a glimpse at his new book. Pound went on to publish a good review, sullied by attacking statements against American neglectful publishers which were not likely to improve Frost's standing at home. Elsewhere the *London Academy* found itself seeking to express "the difference which marks off *A Boy's Will* from all the other books here noticed... We have read every line with that amazement and delight which are too seldom evoked by books of modern verse". Yeats was unequivocal in his praise: "The best poetry written in America for a long time" he declared, and expressed a desire to meet this new poet.

What might have been an important meeting turned into a disaster in February, when on the fifth of the month Edward Thomas, at the invitation of Rupert Brooke, attended one of Edward Marsh's celebrated breakfasts at Marsh's Gray's Inn apartment. Thomas, a complex man of many subtle moods, was apparently not at his best with the sparkling, somewhat superficial society banter that made up so much of Marsh's get-togethers, and was unable to contribute much in the way of graceful conversation. Marsh later put it down to "dyspepsia", although reticence was not uncommon among people meeting Marsh's dominating personality for the first time. Whatever happened on that day, there was to be no further contact between the two men. After Thomas's death, when Marsh was compiling future anthologies, many poets pleaded with him to include Thomas. Marsh always resisted on the basis that he would not, on principle, include poets' work posthumously. When Thomas joined the army he was not recognised at a social occasion by Marsh, who stood within a yard of him with Sturge Moore and R.C. Trevelyan.

As the year progressed, Edward Thomas set off on an April bicycle journey from London to the Quantocks to research for his next book, *In Pursuit of Spring*. His home life had become increasingly claustrophobic. At Steep, near Petersfield, the Thomases had lived in a high modern house built by one of the moving lights at Bedales school, where Helen Thomas taught. Geoffrey Lupton was of the school of William Morris, and although Thomas did not like the house, it must have provided space and air that their new home, the little semi-detached worker's house called 'Yew Tree Cottage', could never rival. It was this that became their home for a number of years after July 1913. As Gibson felt the world opening up for him, Thomas must have been experiencing the opposite emotion. He was receiving rejections from publishers, two of his published books earned only ten shillings in six months between them, and he longed to do something for himself. In short, the creative animal was trying to break free of the critic, however gifted that critic might be. As he wrote to Eleanor Farjeon on 5 September 1913:

> I'm sick of talking and writing about books, and I am trying to hit on a subject — an itinerary or a fiction — I can't yet do an autobiography — which will enable me to put my material in a continuous and united form instead of my usual patchwork. Can you help? [ET/EF p.28]

Eleanor's solution was intuitive and perceptive, and it was to come about a month later, during an October visit to the Thomases:

> One night this month, when I was staying at Steep, Edward gave me a copy of *Light and Twilight* which he had picked up secondhand in a bookshop in town... It was the first of his books that he had given me, the first of his prose that I had ever read. That night in bed I read the exquisite 'Flower-Gatherer', and the two following it: 'A Group of Statuary' and 'Home' — that haunting haunted tale of a young soldier "dying in a far land"... Next morning I tried to tell him, shyly

and inadequately, something of what his writing had made me feel. Then I asked, "Haven't you ever written poetry, Edward?"

"Me?" He uttered a short self-scornful laugh. "I couldn't write a poem to save my life." [ET/EF pp.40-41]

It is interesting to note that the suggestion that Thomas turn to poetry is usually assumed to have come from Robert Frost first during the Dymock summer of 1914. The truth of the matter is that Eleanor Farjeon had planted the seed during the previous autumn.

Meanwhile the birth of the Georgian movement united minds with just as much to share, that in time would also lead to a bringing together of these disparate threads, via Gibson's and Abercrombie's distillation down to a new publishing project, an even more selective scheme, aimed at promoting just four poets. The plan had come from Gibson and Abercrombie, who had thought of a way of promoting their own work through, as it were, a 'cottage industry' project. Lascelles and Catherine had returned from an Italian holiday as guests of Robert Trevelyan, who rented the Villa di Boccaccio at Corbignano above Florence. While there they visited D.H. Lawrence in his rented fisherman's cottage at Fiascherino. "When we were back in England," Catherine later wrote, "and John Drinkwater was over on one of his visits, he and Lascelles and Wilfrid...started the idea of publishing a quarterly of their own poems, with Rupert Brooke joining in the venture. Lascelles and I had been successful in bringing out two long poems of his, 'Mary and the Bramble', and also 'The Sale of Saint Thomas'. So we were deputed to see to the format, and distributing of what we agreed to call *New Numbers*, and to publish four a year at 2s. 6d. a number."

So the process commenced. And that process was a conscious and deliberate one, evolved largely before that meeting by Gibson and Abercrombie, who had decided on involving just two other poets. After due deliberation, they had come down on Drinkwater and Brooke, but it was to go no further than that. As Gibson wrote to Brooke — then on a visit to Canada in July 1913, where the letter found him in Ottawa: "You are of course, too young to remember *The Shilling Garland*". Abercrombie and Gibson had had the idea of revamping the project under a new title, bringing together a handful of writers and trading on the success of the Georgian anthology, although the keynote here was selectivity, as Gibson wrote to

Brooke: "I don't want the rotters to hear of it, until it's too late to include them".

Middleton Murry's periodical, *Rhythm*, on which Gibson had worked as assistant editor, finally folded after a few months under a different title, *The Blue Review*, in the same month. Gibson was not to know for many years that it was through Marsh's generous gift to Middleton Murry that his job had been made secure. Until obtaining his position, Gibson had been scraping a living writing reviews for the *Glasgow Herald*. When *The Blue Review* died, Abercrombie had beckoned to Gibson from Gloucestershire. A cottage called 'The Old Nailshop' had become vacant at Greenway Cross, not far from the Abercrombie's home at Ryton, Dymock. It was from here that the invitation to Brooke had come. The red brick, beamed and thatched cottage was everything a poet seeking rural life could wish for. For a number of generations it had been the home and workplace of a family of nailmakers called the Saddlers. There was also a special reason for Gibson's removal to the countryside. He had been living in a virtual 'cupboard' in premises over Monro's Poetry Bookshop. Monro had advocated the countryside as the place for poets, and at about the same time, Gibson had met a young assistant at the bookshop, Geraldine Audrey Townshend. She seems to have been the victim of faint praise from both Marsh and Lawrence. The former said of her "She is a very nice woman, without physical charm, but very intelligent and as good as gold, evidently a supreme house-keeper...", while the latter recalled "I think I remember seeing Miss Townshend in the Poetry Bookshop — rather lovable and still, one of those women that make a perfect background...". Wilfrid and Geraldine were later to be married in Dublin, and settled in the new Gloucestershire home.

The circumstances had placed another brick in the spiritual structure that was to become the 'Dymock' circle, and it was little time before Gibson and Abercrombie had begun planning their new Georgian enterprise. Just as the timing of *Georgian Poetry* had seemed perfectly appropriate to those involved with its birth, or to those who wholeheartedly supported its premise at the time, so this new venture seemed to be giving birth to itself at a particularly propitious moment. The much-mocked Poet Laureate Alfred Austin had died on 2 June, 1913, and debate had begun immediately as to who was to be his successor to the title. Thomas Hardy was suggested in some quarters. Indeed the fact that his birth date, 2 June, was the date on which the erstwhile Laureate died would have seemed symbolically appropriate to many, but he was also felt by many to be too pessimistic for such a role. Kipling's name also rode high for a time, although Monro countered this by saying in *Poetry and Drama* that there was quite enough imperialism around, without Kipling adding to it any further. In the end, the choice fell on Robert Bridges. Opinions varied as to his poetic abilities. Robert Frost had his severe doubts ("Because our poetry must sometime be as dead as our language must, Bridges would like it treated as if it were dead already") but symbolically it was the perfect time to launch such a trail-blazing enterprise.

*

Just a month after Gibson's letter to Brooke inviting him to take part in the Dymock scheme, Marsh stayed with Abercrombie at The Gallows, ("the most delicious little house, black and white, with a stone courtyard, and crimson ramblers, and low-beamed rooms"). He declared Catherine Abercrombie "a delightful woman...rather Madonna, not exactly beautiful, but very fresh, and very reassuring, extremely humorous and intelligent, perfect wife-and-mother". The boys, David and Michael were "charming". There is, in July and August 1913, a very real sense that the focus was switching to this tiny village — or rather series of hamlets — on the Gloucestershire/Herefordshire/Worcestershire borders. It may have appeared a spiritual and poetic Mecca to poets and patrons wearied of city life, but the reality tested the resolve of the most resolute Georgian. Sanitation was minimal, as Marsh ruefully reported:

> The bathroom is a shed out of doors, with a curtain instead of a door, a saucer bath which you fill by means of an invention of Lascelles' (who was a scientist before he was a poet) a long tube of red india-rubber, with a funnel at the end, which you hang on a pump on the other side of the path — cold water, alas! otherwise I have nothing but envy of Wilfrid coming to live here. [EM/CH p.242]

Marsh entered fully into the domestic life at The Gallows, helping Catherine with peeling potatoes and cutting up beans, and he walked the lanes and fields with Abercrombie, drank mild beer ("delicious and sustaining, but fuddling"), stayed up until one in the morning, reading and being read to by Abercrombie, whose plays

The End of the World and *The Staircase* he declared "both magnificent". Catherine recalled him fondly:

> Sir Edward Marsh was the good friend of all of us, and a most delightful visitor he was. Though our cottage was of the most primitive, you would not have known from his manner that he was not in a stately home of England with servants and amenities galore. The only time he was at all put out was when several wasps attacked him in the bathroom, which was only a curtained-off recess by a huge chimney-stack in the courtyard — and he dared not flee from them until he had got his monocle fixed firmly in his eye and was able to find his clothes. [TL 15 November 1956 p.793]

During the same visit, Marsh wrote to Brooke that both Gibson and Abercrombie were beginning to have doubts about Drinkwater as a member of the *New Numbers* fellowship. It seemed that Drinkwater's intention was to off-load work which he could not place elsewhere. Marsh's view was "to chuck him and get Flecker or (or and) Bottomley". Presumably Brooke would have welcomed the suggestion of Flecker; and it was true that Drinkwater was heavily preoccupied in other directions, notably from 15 February 1913 with his role as manager of the Birmingham Repertory Theatre, and close associate of Barry Jackson. On that night, Jackson had stood on the stage of the theatre in New Street, and declaimed Drinkwater's pseudo-Shakespearian 'Lines for the Opening of the Birmingham Repertory Theatre' to loud cheers:

> To you good ease, and grace to love us well:
> To us good ease, and grace some tale to tell
> Worthy your love. We stand with one consent
> To plead anew a holy argument —
> For art is holy...
> ...May you that watch and we that serve so grow
> In wisdom as adventuring we go
> That some unwavering light from us may shine.
> We have the challenge of the mighty line —
> God grant us grace to give the countersign.
> [JCT pp 20/21]

Then the curtain drew back to reveal Shakespeare's *Twelfth Night*. Orsino had been played by Felix Aylmer, and in the role of Malvolio appeared an actor called John Darnley, alias Drinkwater himself. From then on Jackson fostered every aspect of Drinkwater's varied talent as a director, as an actor and administrator, and as a playwright. The plays would increasingly bring him fame in Birmingham, but also further afield, with successes in both London and New York. By 1913 their relationship had already been a long and close one.

So it was perhaps natural that there might be some suspicion among certain of the Dymock group that Drinkwater was "not hungry enough" to want the new publishing venture to succeed. On the other hand and with commercial success in mind his presence in the volume would undoubtedly help to swell the ranks of interested buyers. In addition to his burgeoning theatrical career, his contribution to *Georgian Poetry 1911-1912*, 'The Fires of God', taken from his current collection *Poems of Love and Earth*, had won praise — albeit qualified praise — from no less a critic than Henry Newbolt in his review in Munro's March 1913 edition of *Poetry and Drama*. So he remained as a contributor to *New Numbers*. Brooke, who had left England in May 1913 to travel in the USA, Canada and the South Seas, was kept in touch with developments by correspondence with Marsh.

*

In August 1913 another connection was made when Gibson met Frost at the Poetry Bookshop for the first time. Frost seems to have come temporarily under the spell of Gibson, perhaps because of the latter's preoccupation with the labouring poor, and at their first encounter Gibson had suggested he bring some poems to look at. In a subsequent poetic reminiscence, Gibson recounts:

> I gladly took from him a sheaf
> Of verse he diffidently handed me
> Saying he'd be obliged if I would bother
> To look it through, and let him have a word
> Of what I thought of it...

The rather patronising air of these lines is perhaps harder to take now than when they were written. Gibson's reputation was riding high at the time, although he probably overstates the fatherly nature of his interest. For a start, Frost was five years older than Gibson. But the poem, 'The First Meeting', is valuable because of what it tells us of the two writers as they were in the autumn of 1913. The poems brought by Frost were among those to comprise his second volume, as yet untitled, but in due course to be called *North of Boston*. Gibson refers to him by name in the poem: "A stranger, an American, called Frost...". We learn that at the time, Gibson was working on "a piece of Northern verse/About the Border-raiders..." and later on he gives us more specific details:

> ...I put my manuscript aside;
> And, when he was shewn in, though still my thoughts
> Hung around 'Bloody Bush Edge' for a brief while...

A little research tells us the 'Bloody Bush Edge' was a long dramatic poem which was Gibson's principle contribution to the first edition of *New Numbers*. So we have time and place coming together in one poem... Gibson was clearly enraptured by "Frost's racy speech/And...pithy commentaries/On this and that..." but certainly there was never any suggestion that Frost should join the *New Numbers* experiment, although it was at this time that the first seeds were planted about the Dymock idyll that was beginning to flower. Gibson introduced Frost to Abercrombie, "A small dark, shy man with spectacles and straight, slightly greasy-looking hair", who wore "a queer little green hat which tipped up preposterously in front". Abercrombie had something that Frost and his family envied to the point almost of obsession: he lived "under thatch", as Gibson was just beginning to do at the time of the meeting. Abercrombie and Gibson made Frost promise to allow them to find him a rented cottage near them in the Dymock area, and Frost, by now out of sorts with London and the literati who had seemed promising on his arrival, agreed to sub-let 'The Bungalow' at Beaconsfield, writing in October 1913:

> When I can get rid of this house I am to go to Gloucester to live, to be with Wilfrid Gibson and Abercrombie. I am out with Pound pretty much altogether and so I don't see his friend Yeats as I did. I count myself well out however. Pound is an incredible ass and he hurts more than he helps the person he praises. [SLRF p 96]

So Robert Frost set himself to seek the idyll of rural England. An idyll it certainly was for Gibson, who wrote more of the Dymock countryside than any of the other poets who were to come under its spell. Indeed, his writing was extremely specific, including several poems about his new home — 'The Old Nailshop' itself, including one in which he dreams the old cottage's past, with the nail forge blazing in place of his own familiar hearth:

> I dreamt of wings, — and waked to hear
> Through the low sloping ceiling clear
> The nesting starlings flutter and scratch
> Among the rafters of the thatch,
> Not twenty inches from my head;
> And lay, half dreaming, in my bed,
> Watching the far elms, bolt-upright
> Black towers of silence in a night
> Of stars, square-framed between the sill
> Of casements and the eaves, until
> I drowsed, and must have slept a wink...
> And wakened to a ceaseless clink
> Of hammers ringing on the air...

The poem was later to appear in the last issue of *New Numbers*. And again, his inspiration is clear in 'The Empty Cottage', perhaps an image of the house as he first saw it, before he and Geraldine came to make it a home:

> Over the meadows of June
> The plovers are crying
> All night under the moon
> That silvers with ghostly light
> The thatch of the little old cottage, so lonely tonight...

Ornithologists familiar with the area would perhaps dispute the line referring to plovers, about which Gibson writes much in his poetry of this period, but the poem is otherwise undoubtedly of Dymock origin.

*

Edward Thomas's work, in almost every way, finds itself looking west from Steep at this time. *In Pursuit of Spring* had chased the setting sun across south-west England, and his only novel, *The Happy-go-Lucky Morgans*, has more than a hint of autobiography about it. The Morgans are a family who live in an untidy Balham house on the outskirts of London. The family constantly dream of their Welsh homeland, and there is a repeated tension between reality — the necessity to survive against always-impending bankruptcy — and an idealised dream which ultimately comes true, when a new life opens out and the past seems "not magical, but enchanted away from solidity...". In *The Icknield Way*, published in 1913, he ends:

> It is a game of skill which deserves a select reputation — to find an ancient road of the same character as the Oxfordshire and Berkshire Icknield Way, going west of south-west beyond Wanborough. The utmost reward of this conjecturing traveller would be to find himself on the banks of the Towy or beside the tomb of Giraldus at St. David's itself.

While this man was struggling to find himself, there were others who were seeking to find him. Edward Thomas was a reviewer and critic whom every writer and poet sought to have on his side, for Thomas was one of the most respected literary journalists of his time. So it came about that the most significant partnership in the Dymock story established itself, in October 1913. One of Edward Thomas's most frequented London haunts was the St George's Restaurant in London's St Martin's Lane. Here he would regularly meet with his literary coterie, Hodgson, Gordon Bottomley, Lock Ellis, Walter de la Mare, Monro or W.H. Davies. The precise date was 6 October, a date he had made to meet Eleanor Farjeon. The day before, he sent her an apology:

> Oct 5. 15 Rusham Road, Balham
> My dear Eleanor, Will you forgive me if I do not turn up tomorrow? I have an appointment of uncertain time with an American just before and may not be able to come... [ET/EF p.37]

Thomas had by now read *A Boy's Will*. It is hardly surprising, knowing what we do of his own internal struggles and striving, that he should have been so attracted and intrigued by a poet who could write such work as is epitomised by 'Storm Fear' and other poems in the book. Frost's time in England — through the publication of *A Boy's Will* and subsequently *North of Boston* — was to be vital to him as a poet. It is however important to understand that these three years from 1912 to 1915 did not turn him into an English poet of the Georgian era. Edward Garnett said of Frost as he was in 1915 that his was "a genuine New England voice, whatever be its literary debt to old-world English ancestry". Certainly though Frost's short time in England as the world moved towards war was indeed significant for him because he related so much to the tradition as seen through the work of Hardy and Wordsworth, for those around him in England, and particularly for Edward Thomas, it was crucial because their friendship — the friendship that in October 1913 was about to burgeon — finally released Thomas to write the poetry that already existed within him. This was of course still to come at this time; nevertheless it is a fact to be considered at an early stage of any examination of the Frost/Thomas relationship that, as Frost himself stated, "I never saw NEW England so clearly as when I was in Old England". From Thomas's standpoint, the revelation in Frost's work was what he might have expected to find — but did not, at least in many of them — having read the principles governing the Georgians, and articulated in an essay by W.H. Auden:

> Frost's poetic speech is the speech of a mature mind, fully awake and in control of itself; it is not the speech of dream or of uncontrollable passion. [W.H.A. p.151]

When Frost and Thomas met, they may have noticed that their eyes bore a startling similarity in their clear pale blue; more significantly it was what those eyes actually saw that created arguably the greatest friendship in twentieth century poetry. The two men met again, at the same venue, in mid-December. Flint was also present, as were Davies and Hodgson.

*

The advance interest in the *New Numbers* project was considerable, with two hundred subscribers listed in December 1913, two and a half months before the first issue. Many of these had come from the poets' own suggestions, but it enabled the project to go ahead with confidence, with Marsh underwriting the first two issues with costs of between fifteen and twenty pounds per volume at the *Gloucester Chronicle's* Crypt House Press. As he wrote to Brooke in the South Seas: "Only the authors hang back. I do hope you are sending them something. England expects from you more than one sonnet," to which Brooke replied in November from the *SS Torfua* 'Somewhere near Fiji...': "I can't write on the trail. I hope I get in enough, to select something for *New Numbers* from. I'll slip a poem or two more into this or my next letter". On 21 July 1913, Rupert Brooke wrote to his mother from the King Edward Hotel, Toronto:

> Gibson has been staying with Abercrombie, and has got a great idea that he, Abercrombie, Drinkwater and I should combine our publics, and publish from the Abercrombies (Mrs A. does the work) a Volume four times a year. A. has done it with some of his own stuff, and finds he makes most money that way... Rather a score for me, as my 'public' is smaller than any of theirs! But it's a secret at present. [RB/GK p.484]

The idea had stemmed as we have seen from a series of booklets called *The Shilling Garland*, edited by Laurence Binyon. Gibson and Lascelles Abercrombie had conceived the plan at Abercrombie's house, The Gallows. The working title for the project was to be *The New Shilling Garland*, later the *Gallows Garland*, and it grew directly out of the Georgian Anthology, which had demonstrated that an identifiable group attracted more attention and sales than a single poet standing alone. Brooke was clearly flattered as well as surprised by the invitation: he admired Gibson particularly, who had a reputation riding high at the time on both sides of the Atlantic. So he accepted the invitation with alacrity, writing to Gibson:

> I think the G.G.[*Gallows Garland*] is a great idea. I'm all for amalgamating our four publics, the more that mine is far the smallest! I'm afraid I shall be outwritten by you fluent giants. [RB/GK p.486]

But he was still able to direct a good-humoured though accurate satirical broadside at the styles of the included writers with an invented contents page:

> I foresee the average number will read as follows:
> 1. Lascelles Abercrombie: Haman and Mordecai. pp. 1 - 78
> 2. John Drinkwater: The Sonority of God: An Ode. pp. 79 - 143
> 3. W.W. Gibson: Poor Bloody Bill: A Tale. pp.144 - 187
> 4. Rupert Brooke: Oh Dear! Oh Dear! A Sonnet. p. 188
> 5. Lascelles Abercrombie: Asshur-Bani-Pal and Og King of

[RB/GK pp.486-7]

Brooke had jokingly estimated that profits from this publication would range from Gibson's share of '£130.10.6' to his own of '£0.10.2.'.

For the group that was to become identified as 'Dymock', 1913 was a year of coming together, and of expectation. Elsewhere it had been a year of progress and drama; in October, Henry Ford had unveiled the first moving assembly plant for cars in Highland Park, Michigan. The implication was that Ford was to manufacture a quarter of a million Model T cars in the following year, bringing popular motoring — and the remote countryside — closer than ever before. In the world of literature, away from the preoccupations of the Georgians and the *New Numbers* poets, Marcel Proust was attracting attention with his new novel, published at his own expense, called *À la Récherche du Temps Perdu*, while D.H. Lawrence, fresh on the heels of his elopement with Frieda, daughter of Baron von Richthofen, published *Sons and Lovers*. Elsewhere it was the year of the Suffragette, with Sylvia Pankhurst defying the police, and Emily Davison dying under the hooves of the King's horse, 'Anmer', in the Derby at Epsom on 4 June. In the Balkans, the situation gave cause for growing concern. The Treaty of London, signed in May, was torn up in July, and Bulgaria marched on Serbia. The Greeks allied themselves with the Bulgarians, and Turkey was also becoming involved by sending a force to occupy the town of Adrianople. Tension was high throughout Europe and into Russia. From the other side of the world, Rupert Brooke, from Suva, Fiji, was writing on 1 December to Jacques Raverat:

> How one can fill life, if one's energetic, and knows how to dig! I have thought of a thousand things to do, in books and poems and plays and theatres and societies and house-building and dinner-parties when I get Home. Ho, but we shall have fun. Now we have so painfully achieved middle-age, shall we not reap the fruits of that achievement...?...Won't 1914 be fun!
> [RB/ GK pp.538-40]

5. 1914 (1)

As one studies accounts of Britain's social and artistic life during the first half of 1914, it becomes abundantly clear that war was the last thing on many people's minds as spring turned into glorious summer. In the arts it was the year of *Blast*, the arts journal in which Wyndham Lewis attacked the smugness (as he saw it) of culture in Britain. In January the Grafton Group, comprising Vanessa Bell, Roger Fry and Duncan Bell, opened an exhibition which pointed to a break away from the Cubists. Meanwhile William Roberts, David Bomberg and the sculptor Henri Gaudier-Brzeska set out to combine elements of Cubism with the love of the mechanical as demonstrated in the work of the Cubists. It was the year of Russian triumph in London, at Drury Lane, of opera and ballet, with the appearances of Chaliapin and Karsavina, and the debut performances of a young English conductor called Thomas Beecham. At Covent Garden in February there was the first performance in the United Kingdom of Richard Wagner's opera 'Parsifal'. There was a new manager at the Old Vic, Miss Lillian Baylis, who founded the Old Vic Shakespeare Company, with the promise of the complete canon performed. There were new orchestral works by Frederick Delius: 'On Hearing the First Cuckoo in Spring', and 'Summer Night on the River'. It was also the year in which the world first heard Ravel's 'Daphnis and Chloe' and Ralph Vaughan Williams's 'London Symphony'. In April Mrs Patrick Campbell scored a triumph in a new play by George Bernard Shaw called *Pygmalion*, as a cockney flower girl who is taught to speak like a lady by a professor of phonetics. Some said that Shaw's outrageous use of the word "bloody", which started quite a society cult, had originated in Masefield's use of the word in *The Everlasting Mercy*. In February Thomas Hardy married for the second time, to Florence Dugdale. Alec Guinness was born, as were

Tyrone Power and Dylan Thomas. Sibelius was awarded a doctorate by Yale University, Burnley beat Liverpool 1-0 in the FA Cup Final at Crystal Palace, in Ireland the crisis over Ulster deepened, and the Suffragettes were everywhere.

Nevertheless for many it was the international scene that held the attention; by March an arms race between the European powers was threatening to run out of control. Lloyd George had referred to it as "organised insanity". Russia stated her intention of quadrupling her army in preparation for a show-down with Germany. In Germany Admiral Alfred von Tirpitz declared that the German navy had grown stronger to the tune of fourteen new major warships in the first ten weeks of 1914, and in Britain, the First Lord of the Admiralty, Winston Churchill, presented a new, larger navy budget to Parliament, stating, "It is our intention to put eight squadrons into service in the time it takes Germany to build five," to which a Labour spokesman retorted, "Churchill's attitude represents a danger for the security of the country and for world peace".

*

> There is a small country road which runs from Newent nearly parallel with the Dymock road, but a little nearer Gloucester, and passes through most beautiful country away to Bromsberrow Heath and the Malverns. Three miles beyond Newent it crosses the Leadon, here a very beautiful little river, very unlike the dirty ditch it becomes at Over... Beyond Ketford Bridge you pass through deep-set lanes of red clay fringed with flowers and ferns to the little hamlet of Ryton, half brick half timber, backed by the happily named Redmarley Hills and in springtime a golden gush of daffodils...
> [JH/GJ October 1933, p.131]

That description of the road to the home of Lascelles Abercrombie was written by a man who was to become an integral part of the Dymock story, through his close association with the poets themselves. This was a Gloucester solicitor called John Wilton Haines, a member of a well-known professional family who had for generations made their name mainly in Gloucester city in the legal and medical disciplines. Outside of this his main interests were poetry and botany. In the latter capacity he was recognised far beyond the bounds of his county as a respected authority; the Bodleian library contains a paper by Haines on 'The Flora of the Gloucester Docks'.

At an early age he had begun collecting first editions of poetry, specialising in the work of the writers most closely associated with Gloucestershire. In order to obtain these books, he frequently approached the poets themselves, a necessity where often a poet would be publishing his own work on a small scale. This practice led Haines to many fruitful friendships and relationships, aided by the fact that his own knowledge, particularly of the flora of the area, made him a valuable ally when it came to identification and information about Gloucestershire topography. He was also noted as a great host, and his society was sought by many who enjoyed convivial literary conversation. Haines for his part was a man who loved to surround himself with poetry in every way, and he seems to have been an amusing and affectionate gossip; Ivor Gurney mentions in a letter that "We spent the night at the Haines's...and reputations disappeared like snowflakes!".

Haines was of value to the Dymock poets as a friend and fellow enthusiast, but also in his professional capacity. There were to be a number of occasions when Haines the Solicitor would be called upon to sort out legal tangles, or to smooth over potential litigious situations. He acted for many of the poets he knew and loved, including W.H. Davies, for whom he was frequently at work, be it in the field of property or finance. He was in short the perfect practical and spiritual companion for a poet in rural England to have. He also wrote poetry, and privately published one book during the early 1920s. His work in this field is variable, with influences from a number of directions, but there is a charm about it that conveys his enthusiasm for the countryside in a simple but effective way, as in this verse from 1916:

Come and look for Moon Daisies
In the mowing grass,
Come, 'though Summer's early yet,
Soon the time will pass,
Soon will fade the golden morn,
So before July is born,
Come and look for Moon Daisies,
Dazzling petalled Moon Daisies.

Haines and his friend F.W. Harvey would debate the relative merits of the roads and lanes of Gloucestershire, Harvey advocating the beauty of the by-roads, Haines the high roads (perhaps this was the professional man in him). John Haines was an early car owner, with a vehicle he called 'Susan', (a point that has confused many a researcher over the years). Haines's poem on the subject of roads shows us a likeable and amusing man with a strong sense of music:

> The little roads, the quaint roads
> That wander where they will,
> They wind their arms
> Round all the farms
> And flirt with every hill.
>
> But the high road is my road
> That goes where I would go
> Its way it wends
> As man intends
> For it was fashioned so.

Haines loved Dymock and the valley of the Leadon for its rich botany, understanding as he would have done that somehow this corner of the county had not developed and changed in the way much of the surrounding topography had done. The scale is grand and yet the fields and orchards are delightfully miniature here, with corners in which might hide the chimney of an old deserted cottage that conveys a poignant image of a "land of lost content". He would have revelled in a richer flora than can now be found, although still hinted at in the daffodils and cowslips of Hall Wood or Yew Tree Coppice and the other woods and meadows of the Dymock country.

But it is in Haines's recollections of the poets who came to the area, particularly in the year 1914, that we have his most important contributions, because he conveys in his accounts a very real feeling of what it must have been like to be in the place at the time, as well as first-hand day-to-day pictures of literary figures who have been in other quarters somewhat mythologised. This eyewitness approach is invaluable when, for instance, we come to seek a picture of Lascelles Abercrombie at home in Ryton. The house — 'The Gallows' — has long since crumbled, and apart from a few broken steps hidden in an overgrown hedge on the steep bank, when I visited the spot, it was as though it had never existed. Yet Haines's word-picture brings it startlingly to life. It was, he writes:

> ...a cottage, or rather two cottages joined by a corridor stand-

ing high above the lane shrouded in elm trees flanked by a
pretty cherry orchard and close against the beautiful Redmar-
ley Hills which at that time were densely covered with larch
woods and edged...with daffodils. It is a fascinating spot, and
the cottage itself, heavily thatched and with a garden yellow
with evening primrose and with mullein, was one of the most
beautiful I ever saw. [JH/GJ 12 January 1935]

The other witness to the Ryton years was Catherine Abercrombie,
who left us an equally clear picture in a published radio talk in 1956:

There the earth is a rich red loam, small hills covered with firs
and birch, and acres of orchards, for we were in the midst of
the cider-making country. The sight of the blossoming of the
apple and cherry trees in spring was unforgettable, with miles
of daffodils pouring over the ground. In medieval times there
used to be a flourishing industry of making a dye from the
daffodil flower to dye cloth and hessian. They were grown as
a crop and have spread and flourished ever since... [TL 15
January 1956 p.793]

In January 1914 Marsh was writing to Brooke:

Wilfrid writes still in the 7th heaven. I am to go to him for
Sunday week in his new cottage near the Gallows. *New Numbers* is waiting for Lascelles to finish his poem ['The Olympians'], I hope it comes out soon. [EM/CH p.266]

The question has often been asked — as so it should — as to
whether the Dymock years were really the idyll they appear to have
been. Certainly there must have been very real problems. The writers
were after all for the most part extremely poor, and there were some
difficulties with the local population, as we shall discover. Nevertheless, as we look back on this brief interlude from a more cynical
time, we must surely agree that there was a quality at least initially
in the air that made the experience special and significant, however
much we may qualify that as the months went by. We must take into
account how much life has changed, and how the world has been
affected by the wars that subsequently destroyed all but the memory
of the world as it then was. As Catherine Abercrombie wrote: "...The
world we lived in before 1914 was so completely different from what
it is today, that the change can hardly be realised by those who only

hear of it from the survivors". Certainly her description of life at Ryton — where there appears to have been no rain or winter, at least in the years 1912-14 — has all the sincere romance about it of a heaven discovered on earth:

> I had a permanent gipsy-tent under the "seven sisters" as our elms were called, and sometimes I would have an iron pot over a fire with a duck and green peas stewing in it, and Lascelles, John Drinkwater and Wilfrid Gibson would sit round and read their latest poems to each other, as I lay on a stoop of hay and listened, and watched the stars wander through the elms, and thought I had really found the why and wherefore of life. [TL 15 January 1956 p.793]

Later, in 1916 as the dream disintegrated, Gibson wrote a poem called 'Trees' and dedicated it to Abercrombie. It contains another picture of the same situation:

> The flames half lit the cavernous mystery
> Of the over-arching elm that loomed profound
> And mountainous above us, from the ground
> Soaring to midnight stars majestically,
> As, under the shelter of that ageless tree
> In a rapt dreaming circle we lay around
> The crackling faggots, listening to the sound
> Of old words moving in new harmony.

This rural ideal was seductive; on one occasion Drinkwater arrived with a sleeping bag, announcing that he was going to set up camp beneath the high elm trees — the "seven sisters" — at the end of the garden. After only one night a distraught Drinkwater ran into the house, alarmed by the sound of something that breathed long and low through the hedge at him. The poet was terrified, and even after it was explained that the offending sound had only come from a horse in an adjacent field, he would not return. As Catherine commented wryly, "as John lived in Birmingham he was not used to night life in the country".

Below this urban/rural surface banter lies a self-consciousness. The core Dymock poets were all basically 'townies' to a man. They came seeking a rural heaven and of course they found it, because in a sense they created it themselves. They explored the landscape with an eagerness that sought — and therefore found — significance in

every metaphor this refreshing rural environment could provide.
They revered the dialect speech they heard around them, and by so
doing they inevitably turned it into something other than it was.
Between 1890 and 1914 a vast number of books were written, published and bought which celebrated a sort of 'dream England', works
by such writers as P.H. Ditchfield, J. Arthur Gibbs, A.G. Bradley and
Stewart Dick. Some are good, others patronise the countryman to an
extraordinary degree; most have about them a romanticised idea of
what living in the country was really like. The image-making was
fuelled by the work of artists like A.R. Quinton and Helen Allingham
with their pictures of rustic cottages and village scenes forever
bathed in a golden glow of late-summer sunlight. It all spawned an
idea of rural life that was separate from its reality. What was an
organic part of a tradition became something rather precious, because it was removed from its context. As today when villages
become dormitories for many families for whom there has been no
continuity of experience with rural values, so in the years up to the
First World War there was a vision of the countryside of England as
repository of an Arcadian myth. This extended to the crafts and field
work of the landscape, pursuits seen as taking place in the fresh clean
air, wholesome and healthy: elements that the Georgian imagination
fed off hungrily. Thus while for the poets all this may have seemed
like an escape to more authentic values, for their neighbours around
Dymock it was all part of a centuries-long struggle with the land,
with the weather and with poverty. Ironically all this, rather than
detach itself from romanticism, became a sort of adjunct of it. The
nostalgia that still exists today for a 'golden age' before the First
World War can be seen to have existed even before that catastrophe;
indeed it existed throughout the nineteenth century. There was
always, it seems, a sense of looking back to what must surely have
been better times. Richard Jefferies longed in *The Amateur Poacher* of
1879 for a way "to get out of these indoor narrow modern days,
whose twelve hours somehow have become shortened, into the
sunlight and the pure wind. A something that the ancients called
divine can be found and felt there still". The father of it all may be
seen to be Wordsworth. William Hale White, writing his autobiography under the name of Mark Rutherford in 1881, said that "God
was brought from that heaven of the books and dwelt on the downs,
in the faraway distances, and in every cloud-shadow which wandered across the valley. Wordsworth unconsciously did for me what

every religious reformer has done: he recreated my supreme Divinity". The poet and critic Jeremy Hooker has made a connection between these writers in relation to the work of Edward Thomas (Lecture to The Edward Thomas Fellowship, Lincoln College, Oxford, November 1993). It may be said that the same point relates at least as strongly to the founders of the so-called 'Dymock Group' even before Thomas came to know the area.

How things had changed! Earlier writers, say in the time of Elizabeth I, had a more realistic view of the countryside; men such as Thomas Tusser wrote advice to farmers, and for the smart set who lived close to the court, country life was a bore, a kind of exile. Field sports were the one virtue. Entering the nineteenth century we find that two of the greatest novelists were the author of *Vanity Fair*, a satire, and the writer of *David Copperfield*, a comment on social ills. Life was something that happened in cities, and usually indoors. In the midst of all this came the French Revolution. This sent a shock wave throughout Europe, and intellectually everything came under question. Wordsworth, living through this time, was the begetter of an urban passion for the rural. Returning to the Wye Valley after a period of five years away, he had written:

> These beauteous forms,
> Through a long absence, have not been to me
> As is a landscape to a blind man's eye:
> But oft, in lonely rooms, and 'mid the din
> Of towns and cities, I have owed to them,
> In hours of weariness, sensations sweet,
> Felt in the blood, and felt along the heart;
> And passing even into my purer mind,
> With tranquil restoration: — feelings too
> Of unremembered pleasure: such, perhaps,
> As have no slight or trivial influence
> On that best portion of a good man's life,
> His little, nameless, unremembered, acts
> Of kindness and of love... [& c.]

As the industrial revolution strode onwards, the contrast between urban and rural increased, and with it the ideal of some sort of "land of lost content". It was this (at least) century-old ideal that the Dymock Georgians chased.

Away from the idyll, the battle for the poetic future went on, and opinions were becoming more entrenched. A friendly argument between Marsh and Lawrence, conducted by post in the latter part of 1913, was revealing, particularly in the light of the later rejection of Georgian ideals by the Modernists. Marsh had attacked Lawrence for his use of *vers libre*, reminding him of the merits of metre. Lawrence's reply is significant:

> You are wrong... It doesn't depend on the ear, particularly, but on the sensitive soul. And the ear gets a habit, and becomes master, when the ebbing and lifting motion should be master, and the ear the transmitter. If your ear has got stiff and a bit mechanical, don't blame my poetry. That's why you like 'Golden Road to Samarkand' — it fits your habituated ear, and your feeling crouches subservient and a bit pathetic. "It satisfies my ear", you say. Well, I don't write for your ear. This is the constant war, I reckon, between new expression and the habituated, mechanical transmitters and receivers of the human constitution. [MLC quoted TGR p.111]

The letter ended affectionately enough, but there was a telling last shaft from Lawrence: "You are a bit of a policeman in poetry". Marsh the entrepreneur was never the intellectual equal of the best poets he published.

By the time the third edition of *New Numbers* was in preparation, the rural dream had evaporated a little for Catherine, although Marsh, writing to Brooke, seems to have seen the setback only in terms of how it impeded Abercrombie's progress:

> Catherine Abercrombie fainted at breakfast on Sunday, and kept her bed, which cast a slight gloom. She is going to have a 3rd child, poor Lascelles will have to review more than ever... [EM/CH p.281]

*

Through the summer and autumn of 1913, Robert Frost, still living at Beaconsfield, had been bringing together the strands that would make his next book of poems, *North of Boston*. In fact by mid-October the title was all that eluded him. It was about New England, so there must be a reference to that fact in its name. Ultimately it came to him in the Beaconsfield bungalow late at night, when he recalled a Boston newspaper's property columns advertising houses as being 'North of Boston'. British friends objected — they thought of Boston in Lincolnshire, and felt this would lead to confusion. Frost did not budge; he was excited by his new work with its quality of speech that had "dropped to an everyday level of diction that even Wordsworth kept above". In fact Frost was at this time making a poetic philosophy which he was later to explain to Edward Thomas. By the summer of 1914 he would be able to state it clearly. At the time of the completion of the last 'Boston' poems, he was already expressing it to himself: "A sentence is a sound in itself on which other sounds called words may be strung", and "The ear is the only true writer and the only true reader".

Then had come the meeting with Gibson and Abercrombie and the offer of a cottage home in Gloucestershire. Through the winter of 1913-14 the Frost family had spent their time at Beaconsfield packing and hoping. *North of Boston* was on the way, but the house was full of homesickness. Perhaps this was partly because of the book's New England theme. Perhaps the theme grew out of the homesickness. It has certainly been true of many poets before and since, that distance creates the right mood for creativity, and to be separated geographically from one's subject is to establish the ideal conditions for regarding it. True though that may be, there were other reasons for discontent; Elinor became ill, and this was not helped by unhappiness among the children. The two eldest, Lesley and Carol, complained about the Beaconsfield schooling, which differed considerably from that to which they had been used in Plymouth, New Hampshire. Frost withdrew them, thus increasing the load on Elinor, who bore the brunt of home-educating the girls. The poet found himself for the first time promising a return to the United States as soon as possible after the publication of his next book. But in the meantime it was his regard for Gibson that made the decision worth the making. As Frost says in various letters, it was Gibson who was the attraction in the early days and the desire was to be at Dymock: "To be with Wilfrid Gibson the English poet for a year", and "The important thing to us is that we are near Gibson". That sentiment was to grow sour before too long, but for the time being it was the spark that lit the fire of Frost's motivation to escape Beaconsfield. "Gibson is my best friend... He's just one of the plain folks with none of the marks of the literary poseur about him — none of the wrongheadedness of the professional literary man". And the newly married Gibsons, fresh in their own rural heaven, encouraged

72

the plan for the move at every meeting and with every letter: "We've been thinking of you constantly, and I'm asking everyone I meet to look out for a cottage for you," wrote Gibson to Frost on 25 January 1914. "The one across the way hasn't a roof on yet, and the proposed rent is preposterous. The agent thinks it will probably have to be offered for less, but we must wait and see. As soon as we're settled we'll scour the countryside for a home for you."

Frost had found a patient potential tenant for the Reynolds Road house in Beaconsfield, but time dragged on, and nothing suitable appeared from Gloucestershire. In the end, perhaps out of desperation, he wrote to say that he'd take the unroofed cottage as soon as a roof could be found, if the rent came down, at which Geraldine Gibson wrote an ecstatic letter to Elinor on 25 February:

> We are absolutely rejoiced...we've been hoping and hoping you'd take the corner house but were afraid to count on it... it's especially fortunate for us, it's so near. It will be splendid.
> [JEW p.163]

But it was not to be. Three weeks later, however, Frost received another report from Gibson about another possibility, at a hamlet just over the hill from Greenway called Ledington, a cluster of farms and associated cottages which also even today boasts a bewildering number of alternative spellings including 'Leadington' and 'Leddington'. The house was on a farm of one hundred acres called 'Henberrow', owned by a family called Chandler. From this point things moved fast, and a week later the Beaconsfield house had been vacated. For a week the family lived above Harold Monro's Poetry Bookshop in Devonshire Street, enabling the children to see something of London. Then they set off for the Gloucestershire countryside that had seemed such a symbol of the Dream England lying in the hearts of Robert and Elinor. They knew very little about their new home, except a name, which they liked: 'Little Iddens'.

*

Just prior to the move, Robert Frost's friendship with Edward Thomas had deepened to the point that there was serious discussion between the two men as to the possibility of Thomas returning to America with the family. Thomas dithered about the idea. He was truly desperate in his search for direction at this time; early in 1914 he had applied for a temporary lectureship with one of London County Council's Non-Vocational Institutes. W.H. Hudson and Edward Garnett had given him glowing references, but then Thomas withdrew his application. Borne out of a desire to do something at all costs to escape from his literary treadmill, he had acted hastily. As he said to Garnett: "Knowing I had to do something I had stupidly pretended to be brave, when really lecturing was as impossible to me as sailoring. Simply fear of standing up alone and looking at a hundred people and being looked at. I am very sorry indeed that I troubled you before I discovered what I was really going to do".

So he stepped back into the world of commissioned books. A publisher had asked for a book with the working title of *Homes and Haunts of Writers* which Thomas derided as 'Omes and 'Aunts. In the end the book appeared under the name *A Literary Pilgrim in England*. Thomas's output was astonishing. In the first fourteen years of the century he reviewed at least 1,200 books, (often in the *Daily Chronicle*, but also in periodicals such as *The Athenaeum*, *The Academy*, *The English Review* and *The Nation*). He was also working on his commissioned books — sometimes in the latter years up to four or five a year. In spite of this huge workload, produced under extreme pressure of time and financial stringency, the prose books he wrote were produced with too much care to carry the title of 'hack'. Indeed, life might have been easier for him had he been capable of lower standards; in his obituary in the *Times Literary Supplement* on 16 April 1917, Thomas Seccombe was to write of Thomas:

> The quality of his prose was apt to be too costly for the modern market... There is such a thing as Welsh influence no doubt: but there is also Welsh pride, and Thomas would be beholden to no man for a penny that he had not earned. His pride in the dignity of letters was intense...his system of writing was almost too intensive, if that be possible.

Thomas himself knew this. In his dedication, to Harry Hooton, of *The Icknield Way* in 1913 he had referred to himself as "a writing animal, [who] could write something or other about a broomstick, [but] I do not write with ease". Other than this, he continued to strive at real self-expression, with an attempt at autobiography in the shape of an account of the early years of his life, a work that would eventually be published as *The Childhood of Edward Thomas*, but not until he had been dead for more than twenty years. In March he visited the Frosts once more at Beaconsfield, and found them full of their rural future in the west.

*

When *New Numbers Vol 1 No 1* appeared in February 1914, the poets represented were, as planned, Abercrombie, Gibson, Brooke and Drinkwater, and from Brooke's pen there was not one sonnet but four. The magazine, unpretentious in its grey-blue paper covers, with a front that declared no more than the words *New Numbers* and the volume, number and date, contained fifty-nine pages of poems, with the lion's share going to Gibson and Abercrombie. In fact the contents page at first glance reads not dissimilarly to Brooke's pastiche. Gibson's long poem 'Bloody bush Edge' — the work he had been writing when he first met Frost — opened the volume, and Abercrombie's 'The Olympians' for which the first issue had had to wait, came next, beginning: "It is in Crete, a many years ago:/ Under a peak that strained in icy stone/ To thrust an endless gesture at the stars...". To the remaining nine pages Drinkwater contributed five poems: 'The Poet to his Mistress', 'The New Miracle', 'The Boundaries', 'A Town Window' and 'Memory':

> ...Because one said — "In memory
> Is half the health of your estate,"
> I smote the dead years under me,
> I smote, and cast them from my gate.

Brooke was represented by his poems 'A Memory', 'One Day', 'Mutability', and his 'Sonnet suggested by some of the Proceedings of the Society for Psychical Research': he was in Tahiti at this time, and received a long letter from Edward Marsh who commented on what might have been an embarrassing typographical error in the printing of this poem:

> By the way, it's lucky I saw the proofs of *N.N.*, they were
> making you talk of griping hands (instead of groping) in the
> SPR sonnet. It's flattering that Lascelles and Wilfrid should
> have been quite prepared to take that from you! [EM/CH p 269]

Brooke had sent Marsh a new poem, 'Heaven', an image of the after-life as imagined by a fish. Marsh wrote:

> I'm enraptured by the fish's heaven, it is brilliantly amusing,
> and also beautiful. It certainly mustn't come out in *New
> Numbers* as all the clergymen would at once withdraw their
> subscriptions!... [EM/CH p.268]

He went on that he had been staying "with the Wilfrids, who seem flawlessly happy", and that "the Lascelles dined with us on Saturday and we with them on Sunday — there is another delightful marriage! with the added charm of children... L. read out his 'End of the World', now finished, and to appear in the 2nd *N.N.* It's a sublime work, in its fusion of poetry and comedy there has been nothing like it... We had a lovely walk, it's beautiful country...".

And so the first copies of *New Numbers* went out from Dymock. The initial two hundred or so subscribers — either individual or bookshop — were by mail-order, and Catherine Abercrombie with a child on her knee, addressed the envelopes, while Gibson made himself pale and nauseous by licking too many postage stamps. Then the packages, franked and posted at Dymock Post Office by Charlie Wetson and Jack Brooke under the eye of Postmaster Griffiths, began their various journeys.

Marsh was delighted with the first number, declaring "the shape, print and appearance quite excellent". And the new publication was a success with the press, with Abercrombie's long poem and Brooke's 'Psychical Research' sonnet being singled out for particular praise.

*

The Frosts' arrival in Dymock could not have been better timed if they were to see the natural beauties of the place at their best. In April 1914, everything sparkling in the spring light, the blossom trees shone, the grass almost seemed to glow after the muted shades of London, and above all the daffodils made the whole family gasp. It was, as Lawrance Thompson has said [*Robert Frost, The Early Years* p.445] a "green and golden land". Abercrombie and the Gibsons met them in Dymock, and gave them a tour of the area in two rented carriages. They made their way through the lanes to Gibson's home, The Old Nailshop, and from there onwards to The Gallows and ultimately to Little Iddens at Ledington.

After the initial disappointment of finding that after all the cottage did not have a thatched roof, they found the house charming, although in many ways impractical. It was a half-timbered structure of whitewashed brick, squared off by black beams, two storeys with a minute kitchen, a hand water pump, a low-ceiling living/dining room and two bedrooms as well as a sleeping alcove upstairs reached by a narrow steep staircase. For six people it was hardly adequate, but the situation was stunning, four miles away from May Hill over the green meadows. Four miles in another direction took them to the market town of Ledbury. The house had a vegetable garden, and orchards of apple, plum and pear trees all around. Fifty yards along the lane was another house called Glyn Iddens, occupied by a Mr and Mrs Farmer, and across two meadows and a stream another house, Oldfields, owned by the Chandler family, on whose farm land the Frosts's cottage stood, and from whom it was rented.

The house was almost at once set upon by visitors, perhaps a mixed blessing for the sensitive Elinor, who would have welcomed a period of adjustment in order to turn the raw material of Little Iddens into a home. The Gibsons and Abercrombies were on the doorstep almost daily, taking the new arrivals out on picnics. Then came the Gloucester solicitor John Haines, with his amateur but expert botanical knowledge and his enthusiasm for contemporary poetry, particularly when it touched Gloucestershire. Haines was an early visitor to Little Iddens; having read *A Boy's Will* and hearing that its author was now in the area, he set off to find Frost, accidentally meeting him in the lane leading to the house. It was only when he asked the American if he knew where the poet Robert Frost lived, that he realised that he need look no further. Haines describes Frost at this time as being "of medium height but [with] a splendid physique and was especially broad-shouldered. His eyes were an attractive shade of jade blue, and extremely penetrating... He talked much and well, but liked occasional silences and especially late at night enjoyed giving long, slow soliloquies on psychological and philosophical subjects". (This is a point picked up by Gibson in his poem, 'The Golden Room'.) Haines goes on, "His sense of humour pervaded all his talk and he could be sarcastic if he wanted to". There are occasionally signs that Frost was having more than his fill of unannounced visitors, but with Haines he could make an exception:

> I object to callers more and more in my old age. In my wife's present state of health I have to do some of the meals (so to call them), but you won't mind that will you? And you will

overlook some other things if we can laze and talk for a day. You must come on the early train and go on the late. [SLRF p.128]

Elinor's 'present state' was largely caused by the strain of setting up house in Gloucestershire, entertaining the tide of well-meaning visitors and trying to teach her children at home, as she wrote to her sister that she had felt at one point — during June of that year — that she had been on the edge of "complete nervous prostration", and it seems clear that her condition had been poor for some time then. Nevertheless she was still able to appreciate the lovely countryside, with its rich pastureland with the dark hedges and giant elms trees, and the haunting hulk of May Hill, with its views of the Severn and the mountains of Wales in the distance.

6. 1914 (2)

On 15 April 1914, the publishers T. Nelson and Sons issued five books on their spring list. They included a novel by Frank Savile, *The Red Wall*, about the Panama Canal, two travel books by Stewart E. White and the Hon. Maurice Baring, on Africa and Russia respectively, and *Science and Method* by Henri Poincare translated by Francis Maitland, with an introduction by Bertrand Russell. Also published on that day was the latest book by Edward Thomas, *In Pursuit of Spring*, an attractively produced book with six illustrations taken from drawings by Ernest Haslehust. (It is interesting to note that in the first edition, the artist is credited as 'Ernest Hazelhurst', although the signature on the pictures themselves is clearly 'E.W. Haslehust'.) The book's cover price was five shillings, and the publisher's advertisement reads:

> In this book Mr Thomas tells of a pilgrimage from London westward in March and April, leaving behind him in town the dregs of winter, and finding full springtide in the Quantocks. It is full of charming pictures of scenery and weather.

In April, emulating his book's example, Edward Thomas travelled west and visited the Frosts at Ledington. He had been on a cycling trip to Wales with his children Merfyn and Bronwyn, and the three spent a week at Little Iddens. While the two sets of children played, the two men began the long walks and discussions which were to continue on and off through that summer. They walked the orchards and the meadowlands, climbed May Hill and looked out into Wales, visited the churches and villages — probably seeing the famous ancient wall-paintings at Kempley — and talked. The field notebooks held in the Berg Collection of New York Public Library show that Thomas lodged with the Chandler family at Oldfields, the house to which he was to bring his family later in the year. The notebooks also give us the skeleton of some of those walks:

> 27 April. 7.30am. From Oldfields walk over the meadow to cottage 100 yards off, through a gate there and down a big convex meadow alongside hedge, past an empty white-washed half timbered cottage with wild garden...then up over another meadow...to the plain church [Preston Church] where Masefield was christened, next to a brick timbered manor farm house [Preston Court]... [Berg FNB 74]

This countryside had a past family memory for Thomas, although at first little more; of it he was to write:

> It was a part of the country I had never known before, and I had no connection with it. Once only, during infancy, I had stayed here at a vicarage, and though I have been told things about it which it gives me, almost as if they were memories, a certain pleasure to recall, no genuine memory survives from the visit. All I can say is that the name, Hereford, had some-how won in my mind a very distinct meaning; it stood out among county names as the most delicately rustic of them all, with a touch of nobility given it long ago, I think, by Shakespeare's 'Harry of Hereford, Lancaster and Derby'. [*This England*, quoted in PET p.222]

It was a landscape that was to become deeply significant, even symbolic, to both men. As they walked Frost was able to explain his "sound of sense" theory of poetry to a sympathetic and under-standing ear: it was probably the conversations begun then that led to Thomas's deeply perceptive reviews of *North of Boston* a few months later. And it was the beginning of a shift in Frost's under-standing of friendship and intellectual kinship. He had come to Dymock largely "to be near Gibson". That relationship was ulti-mately not to stand the test of 1914, while he was to look back on his friendship with Thomas as something akin to brotherhood.

For Thomas it was a vital time too. It should be said however that suggestions that Frost turned him into a poet during that Summer need to be qualified. Indeed it was not something that Frost ever subsequently claimed: only that "I dragged him out from under the heap of his own work in prose he was buried alive under". Thomas had been moving towards poetry for some time, although he had dared not admit it to himself. He was growing more and more out of sorts with the hack prose work of his necessary commissions, and probably the equal necessity of reviewing the work of poets his own judgements told him were inferior and yet successful would have sharpened his subconscious resolve. We know that Eleanor Farjeon had suggested poetry to him, and the thought was present in others' minds too. A year earlier, W.H. Hudson had written to Edward Garnett perceptively that "I believe he [Thomas] has taken the wrong path and is wandering lost in the vast wilderness. He is essentially a poet". In an important letter to Frost written after the April visit, Thomas asks him, "I wonder whether you can imagine me taking to verse. If you can I might get over the feeling that it is impossible". There is no doubt that Frost's support, as he put it, his "bantering, teasing and bullying" released an essence in Thomas. There is equally no doubt that this essence was already in Thomas — had, indeed, always been there. When a gift is so much a part of a person, it can go unrecognised; there can be a certain perversity in the artistic temperament that pulls against the natural course of action. It may be that this was operating in Thomas at this time, albeit subconsciously.

Also present from an early stage in Thomas's critical work is an awareness — which predates the first Georgian anthology — of the importance of a non-poetic style of diction. Right back in 1908 he had said of Yeats's *Poems* published in that year, that for him it was the naturalness of the ordinary speeches in the work which "prove as much as Wordsworth's *Preface* that the speech of poetry can be that of life". Even before that, reviewing a 1901 volume of Davies's poetry, he commended the "ordinary diction" and the "honest voice" of the work. It is hardly any wonder then that when given time together, Frost and Thomas of all people should find such intellectual stimulation in one another's company. The former was already exploring and developing further the theories the latter had sensed more than a dozen years before. What now remained to be seen was whether or not the critic could put these ideas into practice himself. The signs were that he would, if he but allowed himself to do so.

The "undamming" of the poetry in Thomas, as Eleanor Farjeon has appropriately put it, did not happen until later in the year. But the April week at Dymock was an important part of a process which had begun with the first two meetings between the two men in London in 1913. What added meat to the debate was the gift Thomas made Frost of *In Pursuit of Spring*. It is a remarkable book, full of fine descriptive writing, but with another, less tangible sense that gives it almost at times an 'otherworldly' quality. This is aided by the curious device Thomas uses which, it becomes clear as we know him better, is self-derisory: that of "The Other Man", a strange anonymous fellow-traveller who shadows the journey, also on a bicycle, sometimes joining him in conversation, sometimes merely appearing close by. Thomas was later to write a strange poem called 'The Other' in which this figure becomes more menacing.

In the meantime Frost read *In Pursuit of Spring*, and declared that Thomas had already written poetry. All that was left was to show it to be so by dividing the lines accordingly. It is interesting to note that many of Thomas's poems are indeed derived from earlier prose passages. It would seem from a letter Thomas wrote to his friend Gordon Bottomley shortly after his first visit to Ledington in 1914, that this had been the first occasion on which he had met Lascelles Abercrombie. Thomas comments that he is "like Ransome in some ways". The two men obviously got on well, but Edward was concerned about Abercrombie's health; "He doesn't look well", and clearly, although needing to take care of himself, showed no inclination to do so. Thomas probably picked up here the incipient ill-health that was later to manifest itself as diabetes in Abercrombie. Catherine Abercrombie later remembered the dramatic effect of Thomas's appearance at first meeting: "I think Edward was the most beautiful person I have ever seen. It was quite a shock on first meeting him, unless one had been warned. He suffered very much from recurring melancholy, which stamped itself on his face but only made his beauty more apparent". Notwithstanding this, Thomas was to note that she was "a little hostile" towards him as a result of some of his press notices of Lascelles' work, notably 'Mary and the Bramble' which Edward had reviewed in the *Daily Chronicle* during August 1911. It seems that she still nursed a resentment at his attack on the piece, which he claimed to contain "few charms except an evident delight in naïveté". On this visit Thomas also saw Gibson, but there seems to have been a tension here too, once again caused by Thomas's clear-sighted but outspoken powers as a critic. In 1912 he had reviewed *Fires, Book 1*, and attacked the lack of real poetry in it, stating that this was work that would have perhaps been better as prose, or diary jottings, and concluding that "the verse has added nothing except unreality, perhaps, not even brevity". Notwithstanding this, the April visit seems to have been generally a happy one, judging from Thomas's notebooks and his comments on the April days:

> A lovely warm day with Gibsons and Frosts by Leadon... sleek
> bank of thorns and ash trees. First forget-me-nots in ditch with
> Herb Robert... all the may is nearly out... [Berg FNB 74]

*

In the same month — April — as the first Thomas visit to Ledington, two miles across the fields at Greenway, the second edition of *New Numbers* was being packaged and despatched. Edition one had been well received critically by *The Times* and by Edward Marsh, and there were great hopes for the flowering of the venture. Of the forty-seven pages, there were, as before, a clutch of poems each from Gibson and Drinkwater, with only one poem from Brooke and the lion's share — thirty-four pages — being given over to Abercrombie's new dramatic poem 'The End of the World'. Brooke's contribution, 'Heaven', had been sent from the South Seas and had probably been inspired in Honolulu. The poem gives a fish's idea of what Heaven must be like:

> ...Mud unto mud! — Death eddies near —
> Not here the appointed End, not here!
> But somewhere, beyond Space and Time,
> Is wetter water, slimier slime!

The poem was probably born of one of a number of postcards Brooke had bought for himself. Having received a boost of cash, he admits: "I spend it riotously on picture postcards of highly coloured fish...". Marsh initially offered the resulting poem 'Heaven' to Squire at the *New Statesman*, although later (apparently after a protest from Gibson) gave it to *New Numbers*, in time for the April edition. In the event it was not Brooke's poem that produced the controversy but Abercrombie's. Georgian poetry as such was, as we have said, not a movement but simply a coming together of writers of many styles at a certain time. However, as it continued, and as an influence spread between poets, it was impossible that some sort of stylistic unity would not become apparent. In Abercrombie's poem-play 'The End of the World' we can see an example of Georgian 'realism' which was to give its critics something firm to bite on, and a means of attack which contributed to its ultimate denigration. This realism, deemed by some to be just plain nasty, reached its peak in Gordon Bottomley's play *King Lear's Wife*, which Marsh was to publish in the second Georgian anthology. In the meantime, the appearance of 'The End of the World' should have rung warning bells for Marsh, who had declared the work 'sublime'. In the poem, the wainwright Sollers, says:

> When I was young
> My mother would catch us frogs and set them down,
> Lapt in a screw of paper, in the ruts,
> And carts going by would quash 'em; and I'd laugh...

D.H. Lawrence hated the play and everything it stood for, declaring in a letter to Marsh that he had expected much from the work, but had been bitterly disappointed:

> "The spirit of the thing altogether seems mean and rather vulgar," he wrote. "...No, but it is bitterly disappointing..." Lawrence hated the "imitation yokels" and the "rather nasty efforts at cruelty", but the implications went beyond the content of the piece; there was something spiritually sick in Abercrombie which had now begun to make such works "mean and rather sordid, and full of rancid hate... What has happened to him? Something seems to be going bad in his soul..." [MLC, Berg Collection]

Marsh was to fuel the fire by publishing the poem again in the second Georgian anthology. In the meantime Drinkwater directed it as part of a double bill (with Samuel Foote's *The Lyar*) as part of the 1914 Birmingham Repertory season. The drama critic and historian of the theatre later referred to it as a "brief and noisily talkative verse drama...". It was to be a continuing and developing criticism of many of the Georgians, that they sought to include such 'realism' in their work for its own sake. There soon would come a time for other poets classed by many as Georgians, when there would be no need to do so. In the meantime 'The End of the World' is notable for a vivid description of the Ryton countryside:

> The path,
> Of red sand trodden hard, went up between

High hedges overgrown of hawthorn blowing
White as clouds: ay, it seemed burrowed through
A white sweet-smelling cloud. — I walking there
Small as a hare that runs its tunnelled drove
Thro' the close heather. And beside my feet
Blue greygles drifted gleaming over the grass;
And up I climbed to sunlight green in birches,
And the path turned to daisies among the grass
With bonfires of the broom beside, like flame
Of burning straw.

Drinkwater's contribution was a sequence, 'Love's House', beginning:

I know not how these men or those may take
Their first glad measure of love's character.
Or whether one should let the summer make
Love's festival, and one the falling year.

I only know that in my prime of days
When my young branches came to blossoming,
You were the sign that loosed my lips in praise,
You were the zeal that governed all my spring.

Gibson contributed a longish poem called 'The Gorse', three short poems, 'The Greeting', 'On Hampstead Heath' and 'The Ice', and 'The Tram' describing an incident during a thunderstorm. Also among Gibson's poems is 'A Catch for Singing', which reads like a sardonic comment on other schools of poetry:

...Said the Old Young Man to the Young Old Man:
"Alack, and well-a-day!
The world is growing grey;
And the flower and fruit decay.
Beware Old Man, beware Old Man!
For the end of life is nearing;
And the grave yawns by the way..."

Said the Young Old Man to the Old Young Man:
"I'm a trifle hard of hearing;
And can't catch a word you say...
But the cherry-tree's in flourish!"

Set against that is 'On Hampstead Heath', with its air of prophecy:

Against the green flame of the hawthorn-tree
His scarlet tunic burns;
And livelier than the green sap's mantling glee
The Spring fire tingles through him headily
As quiveringly he turns

And stammers out the old amazing tale
Of youth and April weather:
While she, with half-breathed jests that, sobbing, fail,
Sits, tight-lipped, quaking, eager-eyed and pale,
Beneath her purple feather.

In a letter to Gordon Bottomley, Edward Thomas seems to have
dismissed the volume even before seeing it in final form, although
he claims to have read Abercrombie's contribution in proof. "It
seems to me not much more than A. hastily turning on to the theme
in an almost journalistic effort". Thomas guessed that Drinkwater
"must be hopeless in this incarnation", and Gibson "is likely to be
just sending suitable things to the market he has discovered".

*

On 5 May Marsh went to Birmingham to see John Drinkwater's new
play at the Birmingham Repertory Theatre, and to stay with the
author. He was not impressed, writing to Bottomley that "the subject
raised moral problems which are treated superficially". The play,
Rebellion, written and co-directed by Drinkwater, was a blank-verse
piece about a plot against an imaginary throne in which a poetic
rebel, in love with the queen, succeeds politically while paying
emotionally. Among the players was Felix Aylmer, who seems to
have struck up a considerable friendship with Drinkwater at this
time, and even set one of his lyrics — 'Mamble' — to music. By all
accounts the play was a rather poor affair; according to Marsh in a
letter to Brooke "it isn't really good I'm afraid, and his company is
only so-so". In this he was clearly not alone; John Galsworthy had
written tactfully to Drinkwater after reading the play, "To my
humble spirit it's not quite turtle; it's very good mock". At least it
created an opportunity for the *New Numbers* group to meet up under
Drinkwater's roof which they did after the show with, according to
Marsh, only one pen — "Drinkwater's fountain" — between them.
Abercrombie and Gibson were there with their wives, with Mrs
Drinkwater ("A cheery hoyden" — Marsh) and so apparently was

W.H. Davies, who may have travelled back with the Gibsons to stay at The Old Nailshop.

This visit could hardly be called an unqualified success; Frost, in a letter to Sidney Cox dated 18 May, reports of Davies that "he entirely disgusted the Gibsons with whom he was visiting". Davies seems to be have tried to impress all and sundry with his tales of the prostitutes he had spent time and money on. "Lewd and lame" was Frost's description of him, and he attacked him for his arrogance, although generally it would appear that the Frost family found him a joke, with Lesley struggling to keep a straight face at Davies's attempts at teaching her natural history.

On one occasion the Gibsons hurried Davies — who had a wooden leg — the three miles from The Old Nailshop at Greenway to The Gallows at Ryton during a heavy rainstorm until "the sweat broke out all over him". Apparently it was at a time when rivalry between the poets was at its height, and Gibson told Davies that he should be proud because they were hurrying in order for him to spend more time with "the greatest poet in England". Davies's bitter response was "Huh, good thing it's the greatest poet in England". The Gibsons then hurried in to tell Abercrombie that Davies had admitted him to be the greatest poet in the country. "But that," wrote Frost to Cox,"is what Davies thinks he is himself". And the incident also serves to demonstrate that the sense of competition was strong between the poets, and often far from the idyllic dream world of a perpetually co-supporting muse colony where everyone treated everyone else as a brother. There are several occasions when the mist of the intervening years pulls back for a moment and we see each poet in the 'group' fiercely pursuing his own muse independently of the others. To continue with the "greatest poet" debate in Frost's words, "That is what Gibson, or Gibson's wife, thinks Gibson is". Frost acknowledges Davies as a good poet, although he implies that he considers him to be not as good as he imagines: "His is the kind of egotism another man's egotism can't put up with". A telling remark, for Frost at this time must have been on tenterhooks awaiting the first reviews of *North of Boston*. What he most firmly did not want to be seen as was the simple rhyming countryman that Davies took joy in being.

North of Boston was published on 15 May, and the Frosts awaited the first reviews with growing tension. It was clear that in order to make any headway with an American audience, Frost had to prove himself, and on the success or failure of this volume, as he perceived it, hung his future as a poet in his own country. Certainly among the reviewers he had cultivated strong relationships with Abercrombie, Gibson and Frost, all of whom, through conversations, had become understanding supporters of his "sound of sense" theory, and should be trustworthy in its exposition. Ezra Pound, too, was known to be looking at the book. For a fortnight nothing appeared anywhere, followed by an insipid notice in *The Times Literary Supplement*, which came amidst a page of other short mentions of new volumes. Brief as it was, it could have given a sense that something new was abroad in the spirit of poetry. Instead, completely missing the quiet revolution in Frost's work, the review commented as if it were just another book of unpretentious rural rhymes. After that, silence descended again.

It was not until 13 June that the first real review of *North of Boston* appeared. It was in *The Nation* and it was by Abercrombie. To Frost's relief, it was lengthy, perceptive and favourable:

> ...We have heard a good deal lately about the desirability of getting poetry back again into touch with the living vigours of speech... Mr Frost... seems trying to capture and hold within metrical patterns the very tones of speech — the rise and fall, the stressed pauses and little hurries, of spoken language... Poetry, in this book, seems determined once more, just as it was in Alexandria, to invigorate itself by utilizing the traits and necessities of common life, the habits of common speech, the minds and hearts of common folk.

Other reviews followed, from the *Pall Mall Gazette* and Ford Madox Ford's *Outlook*, but these lacked any real depth and certainly did not put Frost's case as Abercrombie had done. The end of June came, and he still anxiously waited for Gibson and Thomas to appear with their verdicts on the book.

*

June 1914 saw the return to English shores of Rupert Brooke, and by the middle of the month he was back in the thick of social and literary life. On 18 June he was with Abercrombie at the premiere of 'Le Rossignol' by Stravinsky, and two days later was staying at 'The Pink and Lily' near Princes Risborough in Buckinghamshire, with Marsh, Dudley Ward, Ben Keeling and Cathleen Nesbitt to discuss a second volume of *Georgian Poetry*. There had already been much discussion on this subject, with considerable controversy over Ford Madox Hueffer's poem 'On Heaven', which Marsh liked, and Gibson and Abercrombie hated, calling the poem "slop" and adding: "if you do put Hueffer in, I think...you certainly ought to put Frost in too. Frost, at his best, is far more genuinely and deeply original, much more beautiful and interesting". In the event Hueffer chose to withold permission on his poem, and Marsh declared that his anthologies must be purely British. From Buckinghamshire Brooke went to The Greenway, to spend a few days with the Gibsons and discuss the next edition of *New Numbers*. On the 18th, he had written from Rugby to Mrs Chauncey Wells, an American professor who had befriended him while in the USA, enclosing copies of the first two issues, expressing pride in the project, and singling out Abercrombie's work for special praise. He also adds that there are plans for him to have "twenty or thirty pages in the fourth number", giving an idea of the advanced planning that went into the production of the journal. We know that Brooke met with D.H. Lawrence and Frieda through Marsh on 27 June, which means that between the 20th and that date, he was at Dymock for what was to be the most complete gathering of the group ever to occur.

It was a period of glorious summer weather. The legendary 'last summer' had truly begun, as Brooke said to Prof. Wells in his letter, "the air is so heavy (but not sleepy) with the scent of hay and mown grass and roses and dews and a thousand wild flowers, that I'm beginning to think of my South Sea wind [as] pale and scentless by comparison!". Edward Thomas travelled to Little Iddens during late June to discuss details of a family visit of greater duration later, during August; it was agreed that they should stay for a weekly rent of three guineas at Old Fields, the farm house of the Chandlers, who owned the hundred acre Henberrow Farm, on which Little Iddens stood. Some commentators have suggested that Helen Thomas accompanied Edward on this trip to Ledington. This seems unlikely. As the poet's daughter Myfanwy has pointed out to this writer, there were now three children in the Thomas household, two at school and one very young at home; added to this, Helen took in boarders from the nearby Bedales School. And although Elinor Frost mentions Edward in a letter to her sister, she makes no reference to Helen, which she surely would, had she been there. It would seem therefore that Edward travelled alone to Ledington on this occasion.

While making the journey to join the Frosts through the heat of that June, Thomas encountered a delay to his train journey. For no apparent reason, the Oxford to Worcester express stopped at a little Gloucestershire village station, about five miles from Stow-on-the-Wold, before eventually moving off again. The station was close to the River Evenlode, and surrounded by countryside, being about half a mile from the village itself. Thomas's notebook for 23 June has a number of comments on the journey out of London via Oxford, ("haymaking and elms") followed by this:

> Then we stopped at Adlestrop, through the willows could be heard a chain of blackbirds' songs at 12.45 and one thrush and no man seen, only a hiss of engine letting off steam. Stopping outside Campden by banks of long grass, willowherb and meadowsweet, extraordinary silence between two periods of travel — looking out on grey dry stones between metals and the shining metals and over it all the elms willows and long grass — one man clears his throat — a greater than rustic silence. No house in view. Stop only for a minute till signal is up... [Berg FNB 75]

The moment was to produce Thomas's most famous poem, and one of the best-loved in the English language:

> Yes, I remember Adlestrop —
> The name, because one afternoon
> Of heat the express-train drew up there
> Unwontedly. It was late June.

Seldom are we able to place a poem in its time as precisely as we can with this image that was to ferment in the poet's mind for the next few months. On this occasion he stayed for three days, from 24 to 27 June, when his notebook records another such delay at Colwall. (This may be Colwall Stone, between Ledbury and Great Malvern.) For the rest, it was "at Ledington with Frost in always hot weather" [Berg F.N.B. 75]. There were long walks and conversation, including time spent on May Hill together. Frost tells Haines of the visit, "We had a day on your mountain...". Again, turning to Thomas's field notebooks, we find the detail:

> Darkish white grey cloud suggesting rain which never comes... Honeysuckle on porches. Rosemary. Roses... The

land 'in good heart' — in great heart... the May Hill view of
isolated hills like the Malverns but even sharper...cloudy mass
of Black Mountains behind... On May Hill a square plantation
of young Scots firs at top and a few old ones surviving from
former plantations — bracken on slopes and one beech surviving from wood that used to clothe eastern slope. [Berg FNB
75]

And it was during these few days that the Frosts and Edward
Thomas spent an evening at the Gibsons's home, with Catherine and
Lascelles Abercrombie and the visiting Brooke. Later — much later,
in 1925 — Gibson wrote a poem recalling the evening. It was something Gibson was prone to do. As with the poem on his first meeting
with Frost, he was many years later (1944) to adopt the same proce-
dure in his volume *English* with recollections of Sturge Moore,
Binyon and Yeats. These recollections were seldom great poetry, but
they sometimes convey an essence of biographical value. And, once
again, we can be precise as to dating of the incident. In a letter from
Ledington to Gordon Bottomley dated 27 June, the day he left,
Thomas says that he "saw Rupert Brooke at Gibson's on Wednesday,
browner and older and better looking after his tour". The Wednesday before 27 June 1914 was 24 June, so we can confidently arrive at
a deduction that the most complete gathering of the Dymock poets,
the summer evening immortalised in the poem Gibson addressed to
his wife thirteen years later, which he called 'The Golden Room',
happened then, on the evening after Edward Thomas's arrival at
Dymock, the evening after the day 'Adlestrop' was conceived:

> Do you remember that still summer evening
> When, in the cosy cream washed living room
> Of the Old Nailshop, we all talked and laughed —
> Our neighbours from The Gallows, Catherine
> And Lascelles Abercrombie; Rupert Brooke;
> Elinor and Robert Frost, living awhile
> At Little Iddens, who'd brought over with them
> Helen and Edward Thomas? In the lamplight
> We talked and laughed; but, for the most part, listened
> While Robert Frost kept on and on and on,
> In his slow New England fashion, for our delight,
> Holding us with shrewd turns and racy quips,
> And the rare twinkle of his grave blue eyes?

We sat there in the lamplight, while the day
Died from the rose-latticed casements, and the plovers
Called over the low meadows, till the owls
Answered them from the elms, we sat and talked —
Now, a quick flash from Abercrombie; now,
A murmured dry half-heard aside from Thomas;
Now, a clear laughing word from Brooke; and then
Again Frost's rich and ripe philosophy,
That had the body and tang of good draught-cider,
And poured as clear as a stream...

If there is a central moment, a central day, that most embodies and commemorates the Georgian poets and their capture of the idyllic English pastoral dream (real or imagined) that we look back to even now, most of a century later, this must be it. 'The Golden Room', dedicated to Geraldine Gibson, was to become the title poem of one of Gibson's collections. We may gather from the poem that Frost was the focus of the evening, which would have pleased him, since we read from interpretations of Frost at this time that he was somewhat antagonistic towards Brooke's charm and easy sway over every group of which he became a part. Tellingly, he once wrote of Brooke in a list of personal recollections: "This boy I have met once... He affects metaphysical sarcasm and would be a later John Donne" [Margin note in December 1913 edition of *Poetry and Drama*, held in the Library of the University of Virginia and quoted in JEW p.153].

A few days later Eleanor Farjeon received a postcard from Thomas at Ledington, postmarked 28 June. The fact that he had already left the Frosts on 27 June, on a trip to stay with some ex-Bedales friends the Hodsons, may be explained presumably by rural collection times, and by the fact that he had posted the card prior to leaving. 28 June was a Sunday, but Sunday collections were the norm then as now in many areas. The card was to arrange a meeting for the following week. He added: "It is splendid here, every day hot and bright". As the postmark went on the stamp, an event occurred in the Bosnian capital Sarajevo which drove the world closer to the brink of war. A 19-year-old student, Gavrilo Princip, darted from the crowd watching the procession of the Archduke Franz Ferdinand and his morganatic wife the Duchess of Hohenburg. He fired twice. The first bullet struck the Archduke in the neck, the second struck the Duchess, who had flung herself forward in order to protect her husband, killing her almost instantaneously. The Archduke died about ten minutes later, at eleven in the morning. Bill-boards around the country read: "Archduke assassinated. Slav Nationalist shoots heir to Austro-Hungarian throne". But it did not seem at first to be all that important. The queen postponed the Court Ball, set for 29 June, until July in deference to the tragic events in Sarajevo. And Herbert Asquith, son of the Prime Minister, recalled, "The murder roused horror and disgust in every corner of the globe. But it was some time before it was realized by the public that a lever had been suddenly pressed over in the vast structure of check and balances which preserved the peace of Europe, and that once that lever was pulled, the machinery of war would go relentlessly to work". Certainly a chain of events had been set into motion on the day after Edward Thomas sat quietly writing his card to Eleanor Farjeon in an Elizabethan cottage in Gloucestershire. For many, life went on for the time being as though nothing had happened. But the machine had been started and things were about to change forever. *The Daily Chronicle*, for which Thomas had reviewed so often, wrote of "a clap of thunder over Europe".

7. 1914 (3)

Edward Thomas returned from Ledington to a desk full of the burdensome commissions that had marked his career to date. A flower anthology was required by its publishers within a month, the reviewing continued, he was planning a book on Shelley, and he intended to suggest a book on modern poets to Harold Monro. The main project of the moment was *A Literary Pilgrim in England*, a book which examined the life and work of writers and poets — Keats, Shelley, Hardy, Coleridge, Clare, Tennyson, Wordsworth, Scott and others in the context of their home environments. The book was divided up according to geographical area, and had eight regional sections, in all dealing with twenty-nine writers. In addition to this, he was struggling to write something he himself wanted to do — the attempt at autobiography, which eventually appeared in 1938 as *The Childhood of Edward Thomas*. It was his attempt at being the writer he sought to be, another step in the mental process which was to culminate so soon in the great poems. For the rest he was writing twenty sides a day every day — "a writing animal" he called himself — and only stopped for one weekend when Frost came to visit him at Steep during July. The two men had begun discussing the possibility of Thomas returning with the Frosts to America, and perhaps taking up some sort of lecturing post in New Hampshire. At this time Thomas seems to have been agonising over the decision, writing to Eleanor Farjeon that it looked like the only way out of the vicious circle in which he found himself, yet at the same time somehow doubting the practical possibility of such a radical move.

As Thomas neared completion of *A Literary Pilgrim* rumours of approaching war were growing stronger. On 25 July Austria broke off diplomatic relations with Serbia, and a day later the Serbian Army was ordered to mobilise. The same day, the Czar warned

Germany that his country would not stand by and watch Serbian territory invaded; nevertheless on 27 July, German troops invaded Serbia. On the 29th Russia mobilised nearly one and a half million troops, to be met with a warning of mobilisation in turn from the Kaiser, followed on the last day of the month by a formal ultimatum.

In London Marsh was continuing with literary luncheons and breakfasts, and actively planning a second anthology of Georgian poetry. The process had begun at Dymock, during early February, when Marsh had stayed with the Gibsons and Abercrombies, and it had been mutually decided that a second volume was warranted later that year. By May Marsh and Monro were in serious consultation about the book, and selection went on through the summer, with Abercrombie and Gibson gently trying to persuade Marsh to include Frost among the new poets in volume two. Marsh decided against it. He had now come down firmly on the rule of all poets in his book being British.

On 9 July Paul Nash, Siegfried Sassoon and W.H. Davies joined Marsh and Brooke at Gray's Inn, after which Brooke wrote an amusing account of Davies's studied rural simplicity, jotted down from memory shortly after the poet's departure. Sassoon's meeting with Brooke left a clear impression on his mind; Brooke came in late to breakfast, wearing a blue open-necked shirt, flannel trousers with bare feet in sandals. Sassoon noticed his hair was brown-gold, and "just a shade longer than it need have been". He also noticed his sunburned skin, his blue eyes and his Cambridge accent. He was also impressed by "the almost meditative deliberation of his voice". It is clear in the account how much charisma Brooke's physical presence generated, and gives a clue as to how such recollections contributed to a cult after his death. There seems to have been an aura which Sassoon felt almost instinctively that went beyond the physical; here was one "on whom had been conferred all the invisible attributes of a poet...a being singled out for some transplendent performance, some enshrined achievement". The sense of strong physical attraction to Brooke by men as well as women is remarkable, and it was sometimes mutual. There is no question but that he experimented with his sexuality; on 10 July 1912 Brooke himself had written frankly to James Strachey of his "abortive affair" in 1909 with a friend from Rugby, Denham Russell-Smith, during 1909. [Berg Collection. The letter is quoted at length in *The Neo-pagans* by Paul Delany pp78-80.] Brooke's description of the homosexual act on that occasion is completely explicit.

The season of socialising was coming to an end, and things would never be the same again. Nevertheless, there was still time for Marsh to take Brooke for a dinner party at Downing Street, where they met Winston Churchill — later to write an obituary notice for the young poet. The next day, Brooke left London for a brief stay with Gibson and discussions about the third edition of *New Numbers*. A remarkable change seems to have come over Brooke during the month between his two last visits to The Old Nailshop. Gibson notes on a postcard, "He has grown up!". Quite what form this altered demeanour took we do not know, but it may well have been due to a fuller understanding, brought about by the company he had been keeping, of the seriousness of the world situation.

Brooke's involvement in the Dymock publishing project had, up to now, necessarily been indirect. Issue three was the first in which he was able to participate in fully at an editorial level, and it is also the edition which, thus far, was to be most firmly stamped with his imprint. During July he was busily engaged in sending out copies of *N.N.2* to friends, reporting that the subscription list had risen to between seven and eight hundred, which "pays expenses very easily, and leaves a good bit for division". He adds that the magazine looks like continuing to succeed indefinitely, and "the more it's sold, the more poetry and less reviews Abercrombie and Gibson can write and the better for the world...".

The journal had always been seen as a democratic enterprise, with each of the four poets involved taking it in turns to have the emphasis thrown on their work. *New Numbers* number three provided Brooke with the opening pages; ten pages of work produced in the South Seas, much of which was subsequently to become famous. There is 'The Great Lover', written at Mataiea:

> I have been so great a lover: filled my days
> So proudly with the splendour of Love's praise...

From the same place comes the poem, 'Retrospect'. There are two sonnets, one, 'Hauntings', dated "1914 — The Pacific", the other written at Waikiki and bearing the name of that place. And the pamphlet opens with 'Tiare Tahiti', written at Papeete:

> ...Mamua, when our laughter ends,

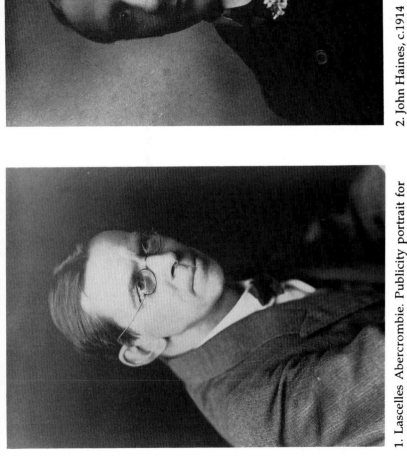

1. Lascelles Abercrombie. Publicity portrait for *Collected Poems*, 1930

2. John Haines, c.1914

4. Edward Thomas, 1913, during the writing of *In Pursuit of Spring*

3. Robert Frost. Publicity portrait for *North of Boston*, 1914

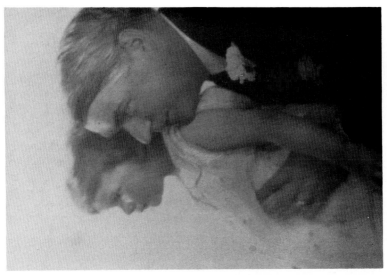

6. John Drinkwater and his daughter, Penny, during the 1930s

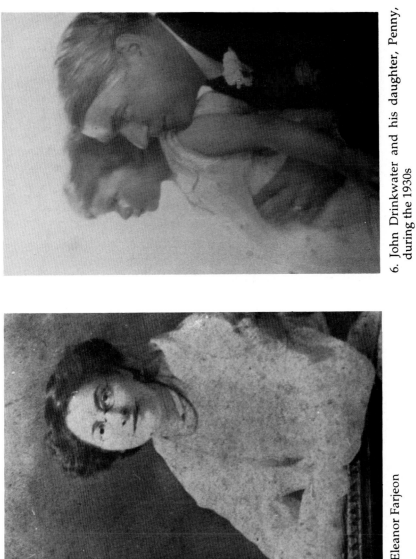

5. Eleanor Farjeon

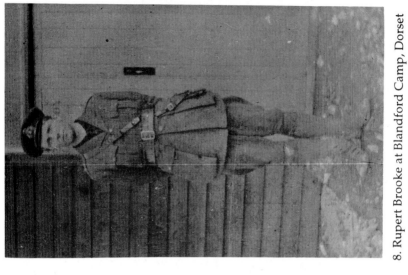

8. Rupert Brooke at Blandford Camp, Dorset

7. Wilfrid Gibson at the gate of 'The Old Nail-shop'

9. At the Birmingham Repertory Theatre for the premiere of John Drinkwater's play, Rebellion, 2 May 1914. Drinkwater, Wilfrid Gibson, Edward Marsh, Lascelles Abercrombie, Geraldine Gibson, Catherine Abercrombie

10. Actors and staff from the Birmingham Repertory Theatre, shellmaking at the Birmingham Aluminum Casting Company, 1915. Drinkwater is seated, left with gloves, with Barry Jackson to his left and actor Felix Aylmer, smoking, in front.

11. The Old Nailshop in 1944

12. Little Iddens in 1993

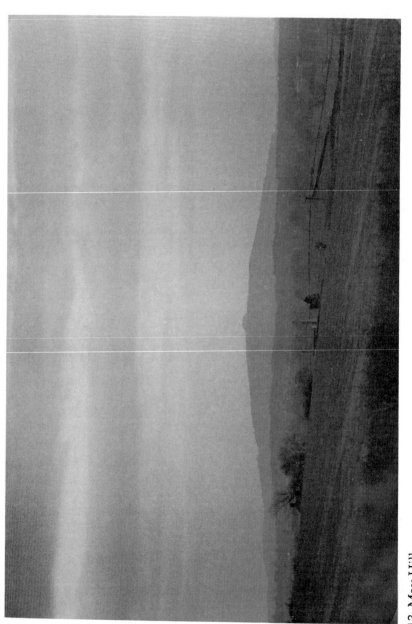

13. May Hill

And hearts and bodies, brown and white,
Are dust about the doors of friends,
Or scent ablowing down the night,
Then, oh! then, the wise agree,
Comes our immortality.
Mamua, there waits a land
Hard for us to understand...

Drinkwater and Gibson each contributed a verse drama. The former was a piece called 'The Storm', the latter a short play set in a circus called 'Hoops'. Marsh particularly liked this. Drinkwater's play was to be performed at Birmingham Repertory Theatre in 1915 as part of a triple bill with works by Frank G. Layton and Ernest Goodwin, and was revived during the 1916 season with 'Her Proper Bride', a piece by L. Allen Harker and F.R. Prior, and 'The Proposal', a first British performance of the work by Chekhov. Gibson's other contribution was a long poem called 'Wheels' while Abercrombie's offering was 'The Innocents'.

*

North of Boston had meanwhile been receiving further reviews, firstly from *The Times* in a qualified notice that ultimately praised the work: "Poetry burns up out of it — as when a faint wind breathes upon smouldering embers...". Another notice came from Richard Aldington in *The Egoist* who admitted that he found it difficult to adjust to Frost's "rather stumbling blank verse...". The big disappointment came with the publication of the August edition of *The Bookman* which contained Gibson's review of the collection. Like Abercrombie, Gibson had spent long hours talking with Frost about his poetry and his style. Yet true understanding seems to have eluded him. It was firstly a shock to find that Frost's book had been squeezed into a corner of a much larger review that included three other unknown poets' work. When he gets to Frost, the praise is faint indeed, and at times actually antagonistic:

> I am inclined to wonder at times if, in his determination to avoid artifice, Mr Frost has not discarded too much. There are legitimate excitements, as well as illegitimate, in the enjoyment of verse; and in reading some of these poems I have missed the exhilaration of an impelling and controlling rhythm.

Was this envy talking? Certainly Frost seemed to feel it was, and a number of latter-day critics have hinted at the same conclusion. Whatever the thinking behind Gibson's review, from this point there was a distinct cooling between the two men, accelerated by events which were to occur later in the year. In 1916, Frost wrote meaningfully of Gibson to Haines: "No sooner had I got down into the country near him than I began defining my position with regard to him — and you know what that means. It means sheering off from him". Gibson's intellect was not of the same order as that of Frost and Thomas; he wrote, as Thomas had said, from the outside. It was little wonder that, sooner or later, tension would creep in. What the Dymock experience taught Frost above all was that he was not the sort of person to be a part of a literary group or coterie; probably the same feeling that Thomas had encountered at his ill-fated breakfast with Edward Marsh.

At the beginning of August Thomas sent off the manuscript of *A Literary Pilgrim* to the publishers, although "who will want the thing now?" was his comment to Eleanor Farjeon, adding significantly "I may as well write poetry. Did anyone ever begin at 36 in the shade?". In fact the publishers quickly responded to receiving the manuscript with a requirement for a further ten thousand words, a task he took with him on the Ledington holiday. Thomas wrote his review of *North of Boston*, then sent off his second review copy to Eleanor Farjeon with the proviso, "If you are worthy of it". Farjeon was staying in Norfolk, but, never one to agree with sea air (and also bound to Edward already by an implicit although well-understood love), happily agreed when it was suggested that she spend part of August near the Thomas family at Ledington. Whether or not Eleanor's love for Edward was ever consummated is uncertain, but there is no doubt that it was very real, and curiously it forged a strange and lifelong bond between her and Edward's wife. There is a moving moment during one of Farjeon's visits to Steep, at a dark moment in the Thomases' marriage, in Helen Thomas's book about her life with Edward in which she gives an account of how this began:

> When Eleanor and I turn from the gate to the house after Edward has gone, I see that her face is glowing, her eyes are bright, and she is smiling to herself, and is so wrapt in a secret happiness that for a moment she forgets me holding the door open for her. She looks towards the hill sharply black in the

moonlight, and waves her hand to it, still smiling, still rapt, and suddenly I know that she loves him. Then, as I stand gazing at her with a new vision, the lamp from the house illuminating her face, she drops her head on my shoulder, and I put my arms round her.

"You love him," I whisper, and though she does not reply, her heart beating so near mine tells me again what I know. I feel again that strange sensation of ageless wisdom and tenderness that I have so often felt for Edward.

"Dear, dear Eleanor, we are closer than ever we guessed we could be, aren't we?"

"Oh, Helen, is it like that, can it be like that?" she asks, raising her head. [USW p.147]

It must never be forgotten that the months that surrounded the Dymock experience were emotive and highly charged ones for most of the participants, with world events playing their part in the time that led up to the outbreak of war.

The family were to be together at Ledington from "the Wednesday or Thursday after Bank Holiday", that is 6 or 7 August, staying for four weeks. Their home was to be the farmhouse down a slope of greensward from the Frost's cottage, across two meadows and a stream, and within clear sight. Edward and Merfyn set off first, on 3 August by bicycle, leaving Helen Thomas to come on separately with the other two children, Bronwen and the young Myfanwy, together with a Russian boy from Bedales who was spending the holiday with them. Myfanwy's eyes had been causing some concern, and she had to see a doctor before leaving. Thomas wrote to John Freeman: "Baby is almost blind after the treatment...she does look forward to seeing what things are really like. So should I, if I thought there was a chance". The Russian boy, Peter Mrosovski, was to cause them some embarrassment on the journey through a suspicious war-conscious England. Meanwhile Edward and Merfyn cycled through the searingly hot countryside, travelling via Basingstoke and Kingsclere, along a route which included "Newbury, Hungerford, Aldbourne, Swindon, Cricklade, Cirencester, Gloucester and Ledbury...". At Swindon the two stopped off to see Edward's friend Jesse Berridge, and while there they visited Coate Reservoir, a boyhood haunt of Thomas's, as it had been for Richard Jefferies, who had set his book *Bevis* there. Edward had written a biography of Jefferies commissioned by Hutchinson in May 1907. It was an idyllic and gentle journey through the English countryside at its most timeless and golden. Everything was so peaceful...

On 1 August the Kaiser had declared war on his cousin, the Czar, on the second the Royal Navy had been mobilised, on the third the British Government warned Germany that the United Kingdom would protect French coasts, and stand by the 1839 Treaty of London guaranteeing Belgian neutrality. Then on 4 August Germany invaded Belgium. Far away from the moonlight of Dymock, there was uproar on the streets of London, and the Prime Minister, Herbert Asquith was heard to murmur in the Cabinet Room of 10 Downing Street, "War, or anything that seems likely to lead to war is always popular with the London mob". And war is what the mob got; as Helen Thomas completed her packing to travel to her holiday home at Ledington, Britain awaited a response to her ultimatum that German invasion troops should be withdrawn from Belgium. The deadline was 11.00 p.m., midnight Berlin time. No response was received, and four years of war began.

The Times of Wednesday 5 August portentously claimed that "This day will be most momentous in the history of all time", and it was on this of all days, as the country began to mobilise, that Helen Thomas set off, burdened down with cases and children, to cross England for a holiday. Certainly all seemed normal on Petersfield station as they set off, but as the journey went on, the abnormality of the situation began to make itself more and more apparent. At Oxford the train went no further, and it looked as though they must spend the night on the station platform. Eventually a train came which was going in the general direction of Ledbury. In fact it took them to Malvern, from where they managed, after some cajoling, to find a cab willing to take them the last few miles through Ledbury and out beyond to Ledington. In Ledbury the cab driver lost his way, and asked a local policeman, who showed great suspicion at finding people out so late, and especially at finding that one of their party was a young and distinctly foreign boy. Eventually they were allowed to go on their way after extensive note-taking by the local constable, through the moonlight of what seemed an enchanted landscape to Oldfields — the Chandlers' house, and their home for the next four weeks — to be met by the figure of Edward at the gate. Today the house has a pinkish hue about it, with shutters. Little appears to have changed since the summer of 1914; it seems likely that when Helen Thomas arrived at the end of her nightmare journey from Steep, she would have cared little for its appearance, and asked for no more than a place to lay her head and those of her children.

And then the sun was shining again, and there was Oldfields hung with greengages in the midst of plum orchards growing fruit for Covent Garden. Little Iddens and the Frosts were at the top of the hill, there was the stream separating them, and there, in the distance, the low bulk of May Hill. A brief, unique time was beginning for the family, though it was fraught as only the family life full of young people can be. The living arrangements with the Chandlers were confining, and Helen Thomas — a proudly efficient household manager — felt unable to organise things as she would have liked. Myfanwy fell from a swing and hurt herself, and the two sets of children, the Frosts and Thomases, were not as compatible as had been hoped. Then, to cap it all, Mr Chandler, an army reservist, was called up, and for a time it looked as though Thomas and Frost would be expected to finish off any incomplete farm business. For a time Thomas and Frost considered escaping on a Welsh cycling trip, but eventually things settled down. From the Dymock time we gain several images of Edward Thomas, and the remarkable quality he seemed to carry with him. Elinor Frost, writing to her sister Leona during June 1914, says "Rob and I think everything of him. He is quite the most admirable and lovable man we have ever known". After the initial period of adjustment, a happy time ensued, with family cricket, "talk and strolling" visits to the Gibsons and Abercrombies, and picnics. Thomas has left us a characteristically meticulous description of his visits, aided perhaps by the fact that the memory of them was to become such a treasure to him:

> In April here I had heard, among apple trees in flower, not the first cuckoo, but the first abundance of day-long-calling cuckoos; here, the first nightingale's song, though too far off and intermittently, twitched away by gusty night winds; here I found the earliest may-blossom which by May Day, while I still lingered, began to dapple the hedges thickly, and no rain fell, yet the land was sweet. Here I had the consummation of Midsummer, the weather radiant and fresh, yet hot and rainless, the white and the pink wild roses, the growing bracken, the last and best of the songs, blackbird's, blackcap's. Now it was August, and again no rain fell for many days; the harvest was a good one, and after standing long in the sun it was gathered in and put in ricks in the sun, to the contentment of

men and rooks. All day the rooks in the wheat-fields were
cawing a deep sweet caw, in alternating choirs or all together,
almost like sheep bleating, contentedly, on until late evening.
The sun shone, always warm, from skies sometimes cloudless,
sometimes inscribed with a fine white scatter miles high,
sometimes displaying the full pomp of white moving mountains, sometimes almost entirely shrouded in dull sulphurous
threats, but vain ones.
    Three meadows away lived a friend...
                    [*This England* quoted in PET pp.222-3]

He goes on to describe the gate and two stiles that sometimes three
times a day he would encounter on his way to visit that friend, with
an old black mare with a foal; he recalls a field sloping rather steeply
down to "the remnant of a brook", with a hedge following its line,
and how the path brought him out onto a lane, up which he would
walk for a few yards before arriving at "the little house of whitened
bricks and black timbers", Little Iddens. There was much to talk
about between Frost and Thomas, not least because the first two of
Thomas's three reviews of *North of Boston* had by now been published. In the *Daily News* Thomas wrote:

> This is one of the most revolutionary books of modern times,
> but also one of the quietest and least aggressive. It speaks, and
> it is poetry... These poems are revolutionary because they lack
> the exaggeration of rhetoric, and even at first sight appear to
> lack the poetic intensity of which rhetoric is an imitation.

Contained in the notice is a line that rings like a bell: "It is poetry
because it is better than prose". Hardy himself would have approved
of that surely. We may see in Thomas's choice of this phrase a
deliberate echo of, and therefore answer to, Pound's repeated insistence that "Poetry must be at least as good as prose". The review is
in a way almost as much about Thomas as it is about Frost. Thomas
has been arriving, through conversations with Frost, but also
through his own thinking, at a plateau of thought that makes this the
only kind of poetry to write now — work that "wrings rhetoric's
neck" and speaks intensely although with the cadence of ordinary
conversation. Had he not said as much in other words, in his book
on Pater (commissioned as early as 1911) when he had said that "It
is the last thing that many writers would think of, to write as they
speak", and that Pater's words "betray their artificiality by a lack of

natural expressive rhythm"? Now in these August reviews, he was truly identifying a voice and a style that he was soon to emulate, from a deep belief in the rightness of the doctrine here preached. Here was the real successor to the *Lyrical Ballads Preface*, as he wrote in his review in the *New Weekly* dated 8 August 1914:

> ...Extraordinary things have not been sought for... yet it might be said that Mr. Frost sometimes combines an effect resembling Wordsworth's, while he shows us directly less of his own feelings, and more of other people's than Wordsworth did... It is a beautiful achievement, and I think a unique one, as perfectly Mr. Frost's own as his vocabulary, the ordinary English speech of a man accustomed to poetry and philosophy, more colloquial and idiomatic than the ordinary man dares to use in a letter...possessing a kind of healthy natural delicacy like Wordsworth's, or at least Shelley's, rather than that of Keats.

Here was a critic in full command of his powers who had the intellectual acumen to place Frost's achievement — and by implication, potentially his own — into an historical context, and make sense of it. It was a manifesto. And in other places, the review explores Thomas's own frustrations: "...He has trusted his conviction that a man will not easily write better than he speaks when some matter has touched him deeply, and he has turned it over until he has no doubt what it means to him, when he has no purpose to serve beyond expressing it, when he has no audience to be bullied or flattered...". There speaks Thomas the writer tied to his commissions, longing to escape into the blue sky of his own inspiration. Thomas's third review of *North of Boston*, in the *New Weekly* journal, continues the analogy with the work of the *Lyrical Ballads*, a review which, although the shortest of the three, was to be of all of them Frost's favourite. And it is not difficult to see why:

> *North of Boston* marks more than the beginning of an experiment like Wordsworth's, but with this difference, that Mr Frost knows the life of which he writes rather as Dorothy Wordsworth did. That is to say, he sympathizes where Wordsworth contemplates...

Thomas was not without reason known as a perceptive and sensitive reviewer. But here that sensitivity is matched and supported by a deep understanding and sympathy for all Frost was attempting, partly because of the conversations between the two men, but also because of the affinity which was recognised by them both, that they were both arriving at the same point from different directions. It was truly, as Thomas had said, a quiet revolution, but it was all the more significant and profound for that: "Only at the end of the best pieces, such as 'The Death of the Hired Man', 'Home Burial', 'The Black Cottage', and 'The Woodpile', do we realize that they are masterpieces of deep and mysterious tenderness".

At the time these reviews were coming out in England, Abercrombie's was being reprinted in the USA in the *Boston Transcript*. The door was beginning to open at home for him, as he had all along hoped. It was as though the war was suddenly far away.

*

But it was not far away. On 5 August Lord Kitchener, at sixty-four still a Field Marshal whose credentials went back to Omdurman, became the first active soldier to join the Cabinet since the reign of Charles I, when he took on the post of Secretary for War. Young men joined up in their thousands, assuring one another that "it would all be over by Christmas", and glad of the adulation in the meantime. Around the country war fever gripped the populace, and at Ledington Mr Chandler went happily off to fight for his country ten days after the Thomases' arrival. Even before that, Frost had reacted to the threat of hostilities by going into Ledbury and stocking up with what he considered "essentials": "The walls," wrote Helen Thomas, of Little Iddens, "were stacked up with ramparts of shredded wheat packets, tins of rather cheap sugary biscuits and boxes of highly-scented soap — the Frosts' idea of preparing for a possible siege". On his trip into Ledbury, Frost by virtue of his 'foreign' accent had attracted suspicion, probably compounded by his association with the Russian boy brought by Helen to Little Iddens a few days earlier.

Helen Thomas remembered that a few days after her arrival at Oldfields the village policeman paid the two families a visit, saying he had received a number of anonymous letters intimating that there were spies at Ledington — strange people with curious accents who had come to the area for no accountable reason just as the war was starting, people who spent long hours into the night with lights burning in the isolated cottage called Little Iddens. The policeman was courteous, even apologetic, but he had his duty to perform in following up any such questions of security. (It may be noted in passing here that exactly the same thing had happened to Words-worth and Coleridge in Somerset during 1797!) For Edward Thomas the whole thing was a joke; for Frost less so. He threatened to take a gun to the policeman if he returned, a reaction hardly guaranteed to calm the situation. In the end Edward managed to placate him, and the whole thing blew over, although for a time there was some unpleasantness when a few of the local louts waged a campaign of stone-throwing at the Frosts' windows. Nor was it the last time that Frost's temper was to fray in the face of local official-dom.

First attitudes to the war and its implications for the poets varied. Frost felt it would mean the end of his English adventure, and that he must return to America in 1915. Abercrombie, writing to Eddie Marsh, appears to have been quite distraught: "My occupation is gone, as completely as if it never were. God knows if anything will turn up. Meanwhile I try to write poetry, which seems ridiculous fiddle-faddle in these terrific times". Gibson was more positive: "I think it is essential to do all we can to keep our flag flying during this triumph of barbarism. And, at least, the more reasonable diver-sions people have just now the better". He was here joining the discussion as to the future of the Georgian Poetry anthology. Davies had written to Marsh that "The arts are out of the question... Of course you can't publish a second G.P. now". Marsh himself had other ideas. He had written to his prospective poets that the idea to publish a second anthology was no more than postponed. The war was a nuisance, but it was certainly not the end. Even, as Gibson said to Marsh, if the delay proved too long, "I expect it'll have to come out as Wilhelmian Poetry!".

For Frost and Thomas, this strange, bittersweet time of fellowship and discovery continued as they walked the countryside, continuing where they had left off in the spring and during late June. And the sun still blazed: "God is in His Heaven all right," Edward wrote, "obviously and ostentatiously". Thomas was close to countryside he knew well: his mother's family had had connections in the border lands around Hereford, and the pleasure of being in its proximity was heightened by the joy of sharing such places as Much Marcle, Malvern and Kempley, the British Camp on the Malvern Hills and, perhaps most significantly, May Hill, increasingly a symbol to both men of their increasing oneness with each other, and with this landscape. Edward Thomas himself wrote an account of those days, as the two men walked while the women and children harvested fruit, an account which was published in the *Nation*:

> If talk dwindled in the traversing of a big field, the pause at gate or stile braced it again. Often we prolonged the pause whether we actually sat or not, and we talked — of flowers, childhood, Shakespeare, women, England, the war — or we looked at a far horizon, which some dip or gap occasionally disclosed...

Later he recalls a glimpse of "a stout orange crescent" of a new moon, and "at one stroke, I thought, like many other people, what things that same new moon sees eastward about the Meuse in France. Of those who could see it there, not blinded by smoke, pain, or excitement, how many saw it and heeded?". This passage was later transmuted into the poem 'The Sun Used To Shine':

> The sun used to shine while we two walked
> Slowly together, paused and started
> Again, and sometimes mused, sometimes talked
> As either pleased, and cheerfully parted
>
> Each night. We never disagreed
> Which gate to rest on. The to be
> And the late past we gave small heed.
> We turned from men or poetry
>
> To rumours of the war remote
> Only till both stood disinclined
> For aught but the yellow flavorous coat
> Of an apple wasps had undermined;
>
> Or a sentry of dark betonies,
> The stateliest of small flowers on earth,
> At the forest verge; or crocuses
> Pale purple as if they had their birth
>
> In sunless Hades fields. The war
> Came back to mind with the moonrise
> Which soldiers in the east afar
> Beheld then. Nevertheless, our eyes

Could as well imagine the Crusades
Or Caesar's battles. Everything
To faintness like those rumours fades —
Like the brook's water glittering

Under the moonlight — like those walks
Now — like us two that took them, and
The fallen apples, all the talks
And silences — like memory's sand

When the tide covers it late or soon,
And other men through other flowers
In those fields under the same moon
Go talking and have easy hours.

Many years later in 1936, Frost published a poem which had been perhaps written shortly after Thomas's death, which describes a dramatic event which occurred while the two men were out walking, possibly on that same occasion. The poem 'Iris by Night', recalls a misty damp evening as they "were groping down a Malvern side/The last wet fields and dripping hedges home...". What happened was a rare thing — a moon-made rainbow in the moisture-soaked air:

...It lifted from its dewy pediment
Its two mote-swimming many-colored ends
And gathered them together in a ring.
And we stood in it softly circled round
From all division time or foe can bring
In a relation of elected friends.

The year after the event Thomas still vividly recalled the experience in a letter to Eleanor Farjeon. It was, he said, unpaintable, something the like of which he had never seen before, "a new toy discovered by Apollo", something "more for a mythologist clad in skins". There is no doubt that the extraordinary weather conditions only served to heighten the potency of the time. Senses were sharp, the place was spectacular and there was something in the light, in the air, that made every moment the two men spent together come alive with a sort of spiritual electricity. On 14 August Thomas's notebook records "with Frost up by Bromsberrow Heath... The curved ridge ahead towards Malvern has a curve like that of Sphinx" [Berg F.N.B. 78]. And further on in the same note: "...on a sharp narrow ridge with yew, oak, hazel, travellers' joy on either side, and down...slopes to the more level park and the great oaks — the air hot and smelling like Bath waters, perhaps sulphurous...". And again: "Great heat:... a hot sun with gold glow and duller purple caked cloud in NW: very hot". On the 17th and 18th he is sitting at Oldfields, looking at "a little window, half glass, half perforated zinc with a wood box between and some clotted cobweb on this where beelike flies plunge in and out and crawl up and down the zinc and die and lie — scores of them". And as he sits, the still air carries the cries of the Frost children at play across the two intervening meadows: "19th, Evening... No wind — voices of the children shouting and laughing over at Little Iddens very clear — we have never heard them there before..." [Berg F.N.B. 78].

Eleanor Farjeon came to join the group on 20 August. Originally it had been planned for her to stay at a temperance hotel in Ledbury, but shortly before she left London, the Thomases found her accommodation at Ledington, only a few yards up the lane from the Frosts' cottage. The house, surrounded by trees and thick shrubbery, was called Glyn Iddens, and looked down the slope to Oldfields. It was the home of a Mr and Mrs Farmer, a couple well-described in her book, *Edward Thomas, the Last Four Years*: "Mr. Farmer was an elderly countryman with bad teeth and easy chuckling manners. Mrs. Farmer was a bulky dominant woman who did not invite intimacy... She had stepped out of a novel by George Eliot, her husband out of another by Thomas Hardy, and they had joined forces midway...". Thus we get a good picture of the sort of human context in which the poets lived their summer of 1914, a sense of affectionately amused respect on one hand, met by a somewhat bemused, non-plussed reaction sometimes tinged by war-bred distrust on the other.

Edward's notebook records: "22 August... With Abercrombie to Tewkesbury... I looked out at the broad towered turretted abbey..." [Berg F.N.B. 78]. "On the whole," wrote Helen Thomas, "the relationship between the poets was friendly enough," although sometimes Gibson's rather precious attitude could be an irritant. Edward and Robert would sometimes be turned away from The Old Nailshop by Geraldine if Wilfrid was in the process of writing a new poem, an act which was treated by the others with "an attitude of faintly contemptuous ridicule", although Helen concedes that "behind this lay a little honest jealousy...". Added to this, Frost's growing disenchantment with Gibson after his review of *North of Boston* would have increased the tension. Nevertheless, there were many happy times; Eleanor Farjeon recalls a "sumptuous picnic in the woods" near The Old Nailshop, with "Abercrombie sprawling at ease and talking freely as he ate, and Gibson, shy and reserved, acting the host as circumspectly as if sitting at a damask tablecloth".

There was another social occasion involving all the poets resident in the area, well recounted by Farjeon. Her landlady, Mrs Farmer, had put forward the idea of entertaining all the writers to dinner. Plans were put in motion, invitations were issued, and huge preparations went on in Mrs Farmer's kitchen. When the great day arrived, and the poets — duly dressed for the occasion — came in, Eleanor Farjeon was there to entertain them with family picture albums at the request of Mrs Farmer, who prepared meanwhile a huge feast of country fare, washed down with copious quantities of cider. Eleanor, already used to the drink through her tenancy with the Farmers, to whom cider was a staple drink, was able to take this rather better than the other guests. Frost had led quite an abstemious life regarding alcohol, although it may be said that Ledington, and association with locals such as Jack Haines, had rather changed that. Nevertheless, it would seem that the Farmers' brand of the local brew defeated all poets present as the meal came to an end:

> Mrs. Farmer rose. I rose, and Helen rose, and Elinor Frost. Mr. Farmer rose. The Poets attempted to rise, relapsed on to their seats, and regarded each other with comical consternation. They were perfectly sober, though exceedingly gay; but the gallons of strong cider, against which I had been inoculated, had gone to their legs, and not one of them could stand without support. I saw Edward and Robert stagger to their feet, clutch each other, and go down; they rose again with great caution, clinging together. On the other side of the table Gibson and Abercrombie were behaving similarly. Two brace of poets staggered out into the moonlight and went hilariously homeward like two sets of Siamese Twins.
> [ET/EF pp.94-5]

Eleanor boasted of "The night when I drank all the poets in Gloucestershire under the table". The truth of this should perhaps be taken with a pinch of salt; whether Eleanor, in at the most ten days, could have been "inoculated" against a brew the poets had been experiencing for weeks if not months is open to doubt, unless the Farmers' cider had some hidden ingredient. On the other hand, Eleanor to the end of her life was well able to hold her drink; in Denys Blakelock's memoir, *Eleanor, Portrait of a Farjeon* he recounts an occasion at the Garrick Club where

> the gourmet in her did more than justice to the food and wine. When, after dinner, I returned from the pay-desk to our table I found Eleanor had been appropriated by another member, and was seated at his table enjoying a glass of old port and a cigar. [EF/DB p.47]

While she was at Ledington, Eleanor witnessed the moment when Frost decided his potato patch was ready for digging, summoning the communal forces of the families around him. All afternoon they dug, until a small triangle of land — which had been no one's responsibility — remained undug. Frost had walked among the labourers, smoking and admonishing them with unsmiling humour to work harder. Now Edward, in Eleanor's words "playing labourer to Robert's boss", indicated the last patch of earth and "jerked an earthy thumb...'Wot abaht that little bit, mister?'". It was an example of the easy relaxed humour between the two men, "and the smile underlying Edward's voice never reached his lips: 'Wot abaht that little bit, mister?' Nor did Robert's smile, bidding him finish the job".

On another occasion Farjeon was present during a walk with Edward and Robert, and gained a first-hand insight into Frost's theories relating to the "cadence" in the human voice, "the sound of sense" in poetry. Thomas had already said in one of his reviews that it was poetry "because it is better than prose". Now came a demonstration:

> While we walked, we saw across two hedgerows a man's figure standing against the skyline on top of a cart... Frost stopped and shouted a question across the fields — it might have been, "What are you doing there, this fine afternoon?" but whatever the words the man could not have heard them. He too shouted some answer that rang through the air, and it was impossible for us to distinguish what he said. But the cadence of the answer was as clear as that of the question. Robert turned to Edward. "That's what I mean," he said.
> [ET/EF p.90]

At the end of the holiday, Thomas went north gathering material for war articles from industrial cities — Coventry, Birmingham, Sunderland, Sheffield and Newcastle: "I shall never forget Newcastle's bridges". Eleanor Farjeon left the Frosts on Thursday 3 September. The time of reflection was over, and in the world beyond the Dymock circle the war raged. By the middle of September Thomas was back at Steep. The time at Ledington had been significant for Thomas. But there had been tensions, both between members of families and between friends. As Thomas wrote to Bottomley: "I saw too little of Abercrombie, too much of Gibson, and Frost daily — our families interwove all day long and we enjoyed many days but with all sorts of mixed feelings". Frost was to be unequivocal in his later reminiscence of the summer: In a letter to Amy Lowell dated 22 October 1917 he wrote: "1914 was our year. I never had, never shall have another year of such friendship". [SL/RF p.220] Nearly four years later, writing to Grace Conkling on 28 June 1921 he declared his feelings about the relationship in even stronger terms:

> We were greater friends than almost any two ever were practising the same art. [PW Vol 13 no 4 pp.21-2]

8.1914 (4)

After the first edition of *New Numbers* it became a practice for the journal to print a list of other published works by the contributors on the inside back cover. As 1914 moved into its autumn, three out of the four poets continued to be prolific, although Brooke was still only represented by the one volume of 1911 *Poems*. Abercrombie had published his verse play *Deborah* in 1913, bringing his published volumes to five. Drinkwater had published a volume a year since 1911, and in 1914 the text of his play *Rebellion* appeared to coincide with its first performance at Birmingham Repertory Theatre. Gibson, who had brought out *Daily Bread* in 1910 and *Fires* in 1912 was now reaching a wide audience on both sides of the Atlantic, and this is reflected in the fact that 1914 saw two new publications from him: *Borderlands* and *Thoroughfares*, the latter containing a number of poems which had first appeared in *New Numbers* including 'The Ice' and 'Wheels'. Of the other poems in the book, 'Solway Ford' proved among the most successful, and was much anthologised. Frost, however, was scathing about the poem, writing to Sidney Cox: "You and I won't believe that Gibson's is a better kind of poetry than mine". In spite of the fact that Frost felt the poem was a good one, and "one of his best", he criticised the technique and form of the writing, particularly "the way the sentences run on". By contrast he cites "the beautiful sentences" in Herrick's 'To Daffodils' and Wordsworth's 'To Sleep'. His frustration leads him to give an eloquent and concise explanation of his own theories: "The sentence is everything — the sentence well imagined... Remember, a certain fixed number of sentences (sentence sounds) belong to the human throat just as a certain fixed number of vocal runs belong to the throat of a given kind of bird". He also blamed Gibson for concocting an artificial story. Apparently he had put two tales together — one of a man who had gone mad from fear, and the other of someone trapped as the tide came in over Solway. These were supposedly true events, but Frost doubted their plausibility: "The details of what he asks you to believe his hallucinations were are poetical but not very convincing". For all Frost's attack it is still, as he admits, a poem of some power, with some strong images: "...Beneath the green night of the sea he lies,/The whole world's waters weighing on his head". It should be remembered that by the time he wrote his letter to Cox, the friendship between Frost and Gibson had ceased to exist in any real sense.

On the day of Britain's ultimatum to Germany, Rupert Brooke was holidaying in Norfolk, although he was ill at ease and slept badly "because I felt badly about the war". The change Gibson had noticed in him had taken something away. Everything but the war seemed shallow and meaningless, and he lacked direction. His depression at the war was very deep: "All these days I have not been so near to tears" he wrote to Jacques Raverat as war was declared. It was about this time that he made his famous remark to J.C. Squire on meeting him in a London street: "Well, if Armageddon is on I suppose one should be there". He gave a poetry reading at Harold Monro's Poetry Bookshop, and then, on 22 August, he went to see his mother at Rugby, to announce his decision to fight. On his return he went to Wyndham's Theatre to see the premiere of a play starring Gerald du Maurier called *Outcasts* — "too foolish for words... I could have written a better play with my foot". Nevertheless there was one high spot which he was able to savour outside of the rest of the audience. In the third act of the play Gerald du Maurier was reading a magazine on stage, intended to be "a French obscene journal". Brooke noted with delight that the magazine was actually a copy of *New Numbers*: "Murmurs of subdued applause from me," he wrote to Cathleen Nesbitt. It was the sort of little touch, an in-joke such as only Edward Marsh could organise so well.

On 15 September he was completing his Commission application form, then he was fitted for his uniform, and on 23 September he was lunching with Marsh and Churchill. Then he was at camp near Eastry, with the 2nd Naval Brigade. There were five battalions in the Brigade: Drake, Howe, Hood, Nelson and Anson. Brooke, and his friend Denis Browne, were assigned to Anson. In seemingly no time they were on their way to France, en route to Antwerp.

*

From early September, the Abercrombies spent a number of weeks away from Ryton, returning at the start of the winter. They had made the suggestion to the Frosts that they could move into The Gallows in their absence, and stay on when they returned. It was a large house and there would be room for both families. The Frosts readily accepted the offer; perhaps the thinking was one of economy over the winter months. There are occasional letters from Frost addressed as from Little Iddens up to the early Spring of 1915, but by all accounts The Gallows became home to the family from the autumn of 1914 until their return to the United States. During the time at Ryton, Edward Thomas returned twice more for visits, once again on his way between Wales and his home. He writes to Eleanor Farjeon on 17 October that "we loaf and talk". In addition to the "loafing" he was preparing an article for the *English Review* on what country people were saying about the war and the effect it was having. He asked Eleanor if she recalled anything the Farmers had said on the subject while she had been staying with them, and reported that "Mrs Farmer told Lesley [Frost] yesterday that the Kaiser's ambition was to eat his Christmas dinner in London".

Jack Haines came over from Gloucester, and had his first meeting with Thomas at this time, as the three men roamed the valley of the Leadon, botanised and talked of poets — Charles Doughty, W.H. Davies and de la Mare. The friendship between Thomas and Haines blossomed as it might have been expected to do between two such men. Haines' first impression was of:

> a dreamy man of slow speech and deliberate opinions, infi-
> nitely interested in little things, and enthusiastic over them. It
> seemed as if he had thought and talked over all the bigger
> things until he was tired of them. [GP no.2 p.13]

It was clear, even at first meeting, that Thomas was at a crossroads; Haines recalled him to have been concerned about the war, but also about what came afterwards: "He believed that the world would be very poor, and that there would be no place left in it for 'luxury' professions, with which he classed his own".

Thomas's sensitive spirit was tested by an unpleasant incident while at Ryton. The absent Abercrombie, by virtue of being a tenant of Lord Beauchamp's large estate, was, like Gibson and one or two others, granted privileged access to his lordship's land, and was able to wander with his family freely for picnics and walks. Any children, however, had to be accompanied by adults while on the land, and Beauchamp's gamekeeper, a man called Bott, was there to ensure the rules were not broken. It may be that while Abercrombie was away, the Frost children had offended Bott by picking fruit without authorisation in his eyes. Whatever the background, the shotgun-toting gamekeeper was a surly and uncooperative person, who brooked no breach of his authority and was well known for his officious and bullying attitude. Frost understood he had inherited Abercrombie's rights to walk the land, but on this particular September occasion, the two men fell foul of Bott in no uncertain terms. As they came back from a walk, the man approached them, and accused them of trespassing. Frost, as we have seen, was not one to take an insult lying down, and himself became belligerent. The gamekeeper called Frost "a damned cottager", and raised his gun in a threatening way. Frost appeared about to retaliate, but Thomas restrained him. The incident appeared to be at an end, the fellow moved off grumbling, and the two poets went on their way.

Then Frost's anger seems to have got the better of him again, and he stormed back to the Bott's house, hammered on his door, and proceeded to give the man a full account of his feelings, and threatened to beat the man up if he should ever dare to be so insulting again. With that Frost turned away, but the gamekeeper came after the two men with his gun, and went for Thomas, standing to one side. A final retreat was beaten. The next day, the local policeman was on the step of The Gallows, handing Frost a summons for threatening bodily harm. Clearly now help was needed — perhaps from one of the other tenants? Frost turned to Gibson, but was amazed and appalled at his attitude. Gibson, the Georgian poet of plain life and ordinary folk, refused to intervene on the grounds that his position as a tenant himself with the Beauchamp estate might be jeopardised. Gibson's decline of assistance on this occasion was the last straw for Frost, and finally ended the friendship. As Frost wrote to Haines on 2 April 1915: "I can't help looking on him as the worst snob I met in England and I can't help blaming the snob he is for the most unpleasant memory I carried away from England: I mean my humiliating fight with the gamekeeper. Gibson is a coward and a snob not to have saved me from all that" [Letter in Dartmouth College Library, quoted JEW p.201].

In the end, the matter was dropped. Haines, a solicitor, was always a useful person to have on hand, and in any event, when Abercrombie returned and Lord Beauchamp became acquainted with the facts, Frost received a written apology, and the gamekeeper reprimanded: "If he wanted so much to fight he had better enlist". But there was a taint over the affair which upset both Frost and Thomas for some considerable time. It has been said that implications of cowardice over the incident helped precipitate Thomas into ultimately joining the army, and subsequently allowing himself to be placed in the dangerous position which finally claimed his life. If so, then there is a direct link between the gamekeeper's cottage at Dymock and the death of one of our finest poets. It seems more likely however that there were a number of influences which increasingly played on Thomas's sensitive mind over the next few months, all of which, cumulatively, had the effect of making up his mind to "go for a soldier".

Also from this time came one of Frost's most famous poems, directly inspired by walking with Thomas, but with resonances for both men beyond the literal. As Edward would show Robert his beloved landscapes of the border country, he would regularly agonise over which path to take, finally coming to a decision and setting off with his friend, only later to regret the choice, and wish he had taken the other track. The poem which came out of the gentle teasing from Frost was 'The Road Not Taken', although it seems to have missed its mark in its earlier publication and readings. Time, hindsight and circumstance have of course given it new resonances, but here we are very close to the two men, their walking and their characters:

> Two roads diverged in a yellow wood,
> And sorry I could not travel both
> And be one traveler, long I stood
> And looked down one as far as I could
> To where it bent in the undergrowth;
>
> Then took the other, as just as fair,
> And having perhaps the better claim,
> Because it was grassy and wanted wear;
> Though as for that, the passing there
> Had worn them really about the same,
> And both that morning equally lay
> In leaves no step had trodden black.

Oh, I kept the first for another day!
Yet knowing how way leads on to way,
I doubted if I should ever come back.

I shall be telling this with a sigh
Somewhere ages and ages hence:
Two roads diverged in a wood, and I —
I took the one less traveled by,
And that has made all the difference.

The sigh with which the poem is told was claimed by Frost to be an affectionate parody of his dear friend's indecision; on the other hand, written as it was shortly after his return to the USA it is impossible to resist the thought that this was a sigh that issued from two men rather than one. Then again, the poem must be taken within the context of the relationship; Frost later warned readers and listeners to take the poem with care, and he was also reported to have said on one occasion, regarding his friendship with Thomas: "His mockery was my mockery, and we felt the same about war and peace". In the meantime the conversations about poetry continued; Thomas had even suggested perhaps by way of goading Frost in his turn into formalising his theories, that if he did not commit his ideas to paper, he would find Thomas doing it before him. Thomas had, as we have seen, been developing his own thoughts independently for some time, as his book on Pater had shown. By 21 October he was back at Steep, on the verge of the first poems.

*

On 9 October Antwerp was taken by the Germans and the British troops retreated. As Brooke marched with the Ansons through the hoards of fleeing Belgian refugees, "moving with infinite slowness out into the night, two endless lines of them," he crossed another bridge in his maturity: "...It's a bloody thing, half the youth of Europe, blown through pain to nothingness, in the incessant mechanical slaughter of these modern battles. I can only marvel at human endurance". Then he was on a boat out of Ostend, and then home with Marsh, reporting to Churchill on the Belgian disaster. Brooke was a chastened, shocked man. But out of that shock had begun to come a new sequence of powerful, deeply felt poems. They were sonnets, one conceived on the burning road out of Antwerp, and the subsequent channel crossing:

Now, God be thanked Who has matched us with His hour,
And caught our youth, and wakened us from sleeping,
With hand made sure, clear eye, and sharpened power,
To turn, as swimmers into cleanness leaping...

It has often been stated that Brooke glorified in war. It would be fairer to say, as his biographer Christopher Hassall has said, that "he celebrated in exultation the discovery of a moral purpose". In this, he was not unlike Edward Thomas, when Thomas joined the Artists' Rifles in July 1915. It is clear that Brooke understood that this new work was to be part of a sequence, not just an isolated poem. Gibson, who must have been looking after the editorial side of *New Numbers*, had obviously agreed to delay the December edition of the journal to allow him to finish the poems, and it was equally clear that Brooke was determined to be represented by these sonnets.

Once home, he had time for a round of social calls, including a trip to his mother at Rugby, and a call on Harold Monro before re-kitting himself out (he had lost all his uniform and other items in Belgium, including some unfinished manuscripts, blown up at Antwerp). Friends noted how haggard and subdued he seemed. Then on 18 October he was back with his unit. By now a second sonnet had been added to the first. By the last week in November he had been transferred to the Hood battalion, and arrived at Blandford Camp in Dorset, weighed down with winter knitting from his aunt in Bournemouth. He was sub-lieutenant in charge of No.3 Platoon, A Company. Two more sonnets had been written by mid-December, and on 23 December, visiting Lady Wimborne at Canford Manor, he was working on a fifth, in a small notebook containing one or two other routine jottings relating to the battalion. He was still working on it on Boxing Day, when he writes to Violet Asquith who had invited him to Walmer Castle, "May I wear my oldest khaki and finish a sonnet?". There is an unamended manuscript copy — probably a final draft — at King's College, Cambridge, written on the note paper of the 'Hood Battalion, 2nd Naval Brigade, Blandford, Dorset'. In fact by the time he was at Walmer, the sonnet, which Brooke initially called 'The Recruit' (he thought it was "fairly good") and the sequence was finished but for revision.

Gibson on receiving the poems on 13 January moved quickly. Everything else was in place, it was only Rupert's poems they had been waiting for, and after all, they had held up edition one while Abercrombie finished 'The Olympians' so why should they not do the same for Brooke? Gibson acknowledged them gratefully: "This is fine! It's good to have your poems at last — and they're well worth waiting for". How could anyone know that of all the poems published in *New Numbers* these would make history? Brooke corrected the proofs at Canford. There are in fact six poems in the sequence, beginning with 'The Treasure', which is an inverted sonnet, the sestet coming first. This is printed last of the sequence in the *Collected Poems of 1918*. The sonnet destined to become the most famous poem of all, 'The Recruit' was retitled 'The Soldier' at some point in the process. It may well have been, as Hassall suggests, the *New Numbers* editors — probably Gibson — who suggested the new name.

So the publication of what was to be the last *New Numbers* got under way. John Drinkwater opens the edition — the largest to date, with forty pages of poems — with a long contribution dedicated to Edward Marsh called 'The Carver in Stone':

> ...He carved in stone. Out of his quiet life
> He watched as any faithful seaman charged
> With tidings of the myriad faring sea,
> And thoughts and premonitions through his mind
> Sailing as ships from strange and storied lands
> His hungry spirit held, till all they were
> Found living witness in the chiselled stone.

Then comes the Brooke sequence; hardly the number of pages he had promised himself earlier, but far and away the most significant publication of all. Next follows another of Abercrombie's verse dramas, 'The Staircase', and finally five poems by Gibson. The first three are slight affairs; it is as though Gibson is trying to keep spirits up with light amusing verse. The first, 'The Orphans' is a humorous poem about two old men on the road:

> At five o'clock one April morn
> I met them making tracks,
> Young Benjamin and Abel Horn,
> With bundles on their backs.
>
> Young Benjamin is seventy-five,
> Young Abel, seventy-seven —

The oldest innocents alive
Beneath that April heaven...

The poet asks them why they are out so early, and they reply:

"Homeless, about the country-side
We never thought to roam;
But mother, she has gone and died,
And broken up the home."

The second of Gibson's poems is 'The Pessimist', an encounter with a puppy seller, while 'Girl's Song' has the subject of a cart taking pigs to market. Then comes his dream of the past life of his home at the Greenway, 'The Old Nail-Shop', and finally a long poem, 'The Shaft'. As this was to be the end of the first volume of *New Numbers* there was, in addition to the poems, a contents list at the end of the magazine, itemising the four poets' work through the editions, with numbers and pages listed. The subscription list looked healthy, the journal was increasingly attracting critical attention, and in normal circumstances there should have been no doubt that the enterprise had been proven to have succeeded, and that 1914 would be the first of many profitable years for *New Numbers*. No doubt, except for the circumstance of war.

*

North-west of Petersfield and Steep in Hampshire, the road winds up Stoner Hill, with a sheer drop on one side, offering thick banks of foliage, and beyond them stunning views in which the sky sweeps in from all sides. But today the attentive driver has little time to examine them, because the road twists like an alpine pass, thick beech trees overhead, the next bend seldom more than twenty yards away. That is until suddenly, almost without warning, the landscape opens up and places a high plateau before the traveller. It is one of those places where one feels as though one is high, even if one did not realise it before. The road, like the landscape, opens up and straightens, and two or so miles along there is a crossroads and an empty inn sign by the side of the road. This is the Froxfield Plateau in the parish of Priors Dean. Behind the strange inn sign is a field, and in the middle of the field a low white unprepossessing building, partly sheltered by beech trees. The trees at least are noticeable: there are not that many in this wide open place. This is the White Horse public house, known by scores of travellers for obvious reasons as "The Pub with No Name". The reason for the Inn's isolation is easy to explain; before the enclosure, a road from Alton to Petersfield across the plateau ran past the place. There was a smithy — now a bar — and a pond (still there) while the inn itself is now stranded a field away from the present road, and has to be approached up a rough track. On 16 November Edward Thomas, listless, anxious, seeking a direction, and tentatively edging towards poetry, called here, and settled down for a drink. 16 November 1914 was a day on which the beech trees rushed and roared, although it does not take much to make them do that in this high landscape. There was a girl working in the bar, and Thomas started talking to her. As was his habit, he began making notes as she talked. It may have been that he still gathered material for war articles. On the other hand, he may have done so with another specific purpose in mind. Whatever the motive, he did what every good travel writer and diarist should do, he wrote down what he heard and saw verbatim, not troubling to make judgements or add emotion at the time:

> "I should like to wring the old girl's neck for coming away here." So said the woman who fetched my beer when I found myself at the inn first. She was a daughter of the house, fresh from a long absence in service in London, a bright wildish slattern with a cockney accent and her hair half down. She spoke angrily. If she did not get away before long, she said, "she would go mad with the loneliness". [LML quoted ETCB, pp.163-6]

It was the sort of note-taking interview he must have conducted a thousand times. He wrote his notes with a practised hand, complete with direct speech. In his field notebook for 27 November, he is at Ryton and noting "Clothes on the line violently blowing in the wind and crackle like a rising woodfire" [Berg F.N.B. 79], a phrase that is almost the finished product even before it appears in the poem: "And the linen crackles on the line/like a woodfire rising". On the left-hand side of the page, opposite an entry dated 2 November, but perhaps written later, the poem is beginning to take shape:

> I could wring the old girl's neck
> That put it here

A public house! (Charcoal burner)
by bringing up and quite outdoing
The idea of London
Two woods around and never a road in sight
Trees roaring like a train without an end
But she's dead long ago
Only a motorist from far away
Or marketers in carts once a fortnight
Or a few fresh tramps ignorant
of the house turning.
[Berg F.N.B. 79]

The next page, undated, has a short list headed 'Subjects', and including 'The White Horse'. By 3 December the first poem, 'Up in the Wind' was complete:

"I could wring the old thing's neck that put it there!
A public house! it may be public for birds,
Squirrels, and such-like, ghosts of charcoal burners
And highwaymen." The wild girl laughed. "But I
Hate it since I came back from Kennington.
I gave up a good place..."

The flood-gates had been opened, the "undamming" had begun. His own instincts, Frost's encouragings, and the long Dymock walks, bore fruit at last. He had adopted the technique suggested by Frost, that of working from a prose sketch, and the result was instant success. A day later he had written 'November Sky', and the next day 'March'. On 6 December came 'Old Man', based on the Southern-wood herb that grew in a clump outside his door at Steep, and which his daughter Myfanwy used to pick absentmindedly. Finally, in this astonishing first outpouring, came 'The Sign Post' on 7 December. A week later he was confident enough to write to Frost at Ryton that he was "in it and no mistake", and sent copies of the first poems, of which Frost liked 'Old Man' best. But it almost seemed not to matter now. There was a belief in Thomas that was tantamount to total conviction, probably for the first time in his entire life. He knew he was at last himself in these poems. The duty-writing had not gone away: he was about to plunge into a biography, *The Life of the Duke of Marlborough*, and he was still anguishing about the war. Inter-estingly though, even by the end of 1914 he had not given up the idea of possibly going to America with Frost. It was as though these decisions, which had been hanging over him, could now be made in their own time. What mattered now was the new-found perfection of his poems. Before the end of the year he had written his long poem 'The Other', with its sinister doppelganger version of the figure in *In Pursuit of Spring*. The poem, 110 lines long, is full of foreboding, but it begins with what is almost a metaphor for this new situation:

> The forest ended. Glad I was
> To feel the light, and hear the hum
> Of bees, and smell the drying grass
> And the sweet mint, because I had come
> To an end of forest...

9. A Crack in a Wall

At Birmingham Repertory Theatre the war, predictably, had had a serious effect both on audiences and on morale. The theatre in its permanent form had only been functioning for about eighteen months, and had already produced some exciting things. Now the war had come, members of the stalwart Company were enlisting, and audiences fell away alarmingly. Barry Jackson and his manager John Drinkwater tried various combinations of plays in order to entice the public to Station Street. Among the victims of the lull had been Lascelles Abercrombie's 'The End of the World'; the management hired an orchestra, a pianist and a string quartet in their attempts at audience-building. It was the same story all over the country; for the time being, the public could think of only one thing. Then in the spring of 1915 the tide began to turn. The war had not ended by Christmas, as the early forecasts had promised, and people settled back into something like a routine again. Drinkwater's *The Storm* proved a great hit, with Cecily Byrne and Ion Swinley in the leading roles. Two years later Drinkwater was to publish the work in a collection entitled *Pawns: Three Poetic Plays*, but in the meantime it became a great favourite with Birmingham audiences. The play was dedicated to Barry Jackson, who designed the set. At publication, Drinkwater boasted that here was not a play written from the desk only, not simply a literary work, but a piece of stage-crafted poetry, a product of his experience in the practical theatre. This may explain its success with audiences. It is a tragic story of a young wife who waits for her husband to return from the storm, fearing all the time to believe the tragic truth; she is confronted by a strange young man, eloquently praising the storm for its glory. Drinkwater's play had the audiences agog. At the time he wrote:

For nearly two hundred years in England the poets very
rightly have refused to work for a theatre that has sacrificed
the drama to the actor instead of so training actors that they
could give the poet the supreme joy of seeing his work nobly
and tenderly interpreted. [JCT p.35]

Drinkwater counted himself and his plays fortunate in having Birmingham as their developing ground. He wrote of:

...the great good fortune of being shaped in a theatre in which,
of a hundred plays produced in four years [going back to the
first foundations] not five would fail to satisfy a jury composed, let us say, of Shakespeare and Congreve and Synge,
not, of course, as to their greatness, but at least as to their
artistic integrity. Barry Jackson's Repertory Theatre has
created an audience in Birmingham which in the decision as
to the worth of a play has not, I believe, its peer in England.
[JCT p.35]

Throughout 1915 the theatre maintained its performance schedule,
while each Sunday actors and staff worked at the Birmingham
Aluminium Casting Company, making shell cases. No one was
exempt, and Drinkwater and Jackson, together with leading actors
Swinley and Felix Aylmer all proudly posed for a photograph
during their labours. In January Brooke had written to Drinkwater
from Blandford:

Come and die. It'll be great fun. And there's great health in
the preparation. The theatre's no place, now. If you stay there
you'll not be able to start afresh with us all when we come
back. [RB/GK p.655]

*

"We think of home all the time," wrote Frost during the late winter
months. Finally a passage had been booked from Liverpool on a liner
called the *St Paul*. She was an American vessel: he had debated as to
which line he should travel on, but the safety factor mitigated in his
mind against a British ship. The journey was set for 13 February;
Edward Thomas was not to be there, although Merfyn was to
accompany the Frosts. The last three months in England were not
happy ones for Frost. He seems to have suffered from recurring
bouts of influenza, Elinor was run down, and the children did not

get on well with the Abercrombie offspring or with the local boys and girls of Ryton. The Abercrombies were back at The Gallows from the middle of November 1914, and from then on the house, or rather houses, were full almost to bursting point, a fact which could not have eased the tension. There is even a suggestion that Thomas returned for one last visit, although this is uncertain. Nevertheless, Catherine Abercrombie noted surprisingly that "nothing seemed to daunt [Elinor] — she kept her precious metal coffee pot going all day on the stove, and imbibed more coffee in a day than I did in a month". In fact, as always with the Frost marital relationship, there was an inner tension. It was something similar to the sometimes tormented love between Edward and Helen Thomas, in which there seem to have been times when the woman gave so much of herself as to incur a guilty resentment in the man. Elinor's desire to "live under thatch" during the Ryton months was at last fulfilled at almost the eleventh hour of their English time. It was also to give, through a particular poem, an insight into the Frosts's complicated relationship. The poem, 'The Thatch', must surely be about winter 1914-15 at The Gallows:

> Out alone in the winter rain,
> Intent on giving and taking pain,
> But never was I far out of sight
> Of a certain upper-window light,
> The light was what it was all about:
> I would not go in till the light went out,
> It would not go out till I came in.
> Well, we should see which one would win...

Frost goes on to give us more clues about the location through a heart-rendingly personal poem; he speaks of "the thick old thatch", and we see him passing "along the eaves,/So low I brushed the straw with my sleeves": it is a poem of Ryton, written many years after being there, and it ends:

> They tell me the cottage where we dwelt,
> Its wind-torn thatch now goes unmended;
> Its life of hundreds of years has ended
> By letting the rain I knew outdoors
> In on to the upper chamber floors.

The poem appeared in Frost's 1928 collection *West-Running Brook*.

At first the war seemed remote, but attitudes changed, and brought with the change a paranoia of suspicion among some of the local people similar to that experienced by Frost at Ledington. A Dutchman, Van Doorn, visited for a time, and his accent and large black beard was enough to excite some of the neighbours to contact the police, while an ailing and eccentric artist friend of Abercrombie's was also suspected. By all accounts she was partially paralysed, and was "all wasted to nothing". But, as Frost wrote to Sidney Cox, "as the country folk remember her she might well have been a German officer in disguise".

North of Boston was to be published in America, but in a very small edition, and to secure his passage Frost borrowed from Haines, Abercrombie and another friend, J.C. Smith. It was a tense time everywhere. There were fears of a German invasion; on the south coast Brooke's battalion had sighted what was thought to be a German ship on the horizon, and there was a very real alert, although it turned out to be a only false alarm. A naval blockade was about to come into force, and it was a question of time before things got worse. At last the war was visible even in the lanes around Dymock, with wounded, home on leave, mingling with new young conscripts leaving the orchard-fields for the local headquarters in Ledbury, thence to the Front, "soldiers swarming over everything", as Frost noted. Conditions were hardly conducive to the writing of poetry, but Frost did begin work on 'The Road Not Taken' at Ryton, and also another poem, 'The Sound of Trees', said to be about the "seven sisters" elms visible from the Abercrombie's garden, although John Haines recounts Frost stating that he combined the image with a remembered wood in New Hampshire. Whatever the exact truth, there is no doubt as to the dedication to Abercrombie. And there is something akin to the mood of Thomas's 'Up in the Wind' that echoes the disquieting mood engendered by the rushing of the wind in treetops:

> I wonder about the trees.
> Why do we wish to bear
> Forever the noise of these
> More than another noise
> So close to our dwelling place?
> We suffer them by the day
> Till we lose all measure of pace,
> And fixity in our joys,

And acquire a listening air...

As January ended packing began in earnest, with the Frost family staying at Ryton with interludes at Oldfields with the Chandlers, giving them furniture as rent. Time began to run out, and there were many friends to say goodbye to, including the Thomases at Steep, and two nights with John Haines in Gloucester. And there was one more visit from Eleanor Farjeon, who came to Ryton at the Frosts' invitation for a week at the beginning of February, (although in Eleanor's original notes for her introduction to Frost's book for children, *You Come Too*, she speaks of the visit as being in January). In any event it was while they were in the midst of packing to go home. It was, as Eleanor later wrote, "a week of snow in which the friendship deepened" [EF/YCT p.10]. By being present at this last moment, Eleanor was honouring a request from the Frosts for her to join them at Ryton that had been made as far back as the previous August. From this it becomes clear that the plan to occupy The Gallows during this last winter had been long thought out.

Things became more worrying when the Germans introduced the threatened blockade of the British Isles during early February, declaring the waters to be a war zone. The blockade came into effect five days after the Frosts sailed for America, and the first allied casualty was sunk by a German submarine off Folkestone the next day.

After a last night on British soil spent in Liverpool, the family set sail under cover of darkness on the *St Paul*, which joined a convoy, guarded by two destroyers, and including the giant luxury liner *Lusitania*, to travel round the coast of Ireland on a rough but safe nine day journey to New York. On 8 May, again America-bound, the *Lusitania* went down off the Old Head of Kinsale near the southern tip of Ireland, with the loss of 1,400 lives.

*

Almost as soon as the poems started to flow Edward Thomas began to send copies to friends. Nevertheless, he was adamant that any publication should be done pseudonymously, and the few poems that were to appear during his lifetime, did so under the name 'Edward Eastaway', seen by some as yet another search for an identity, but probably because as a well-known literary figure he wanted the poems to be judged on their own ground. Not everyone liked the poems, although Thomas did not seem to be worried by any rejection, so sure was he of his work in this field already. He sent some to Monro, not declaring his interest in them. Monro may well have guessed their source, but he returned them within a week. But then a few months earlier the same editor had rejected Eliot's 'The Love Song of J. Alfred Prufrock', calling it "absolutely inane". A similar reaction came from a number of other publishers, and nothing appeared in print. Some of the friends to whom he had sent copies were also less than enthusiastic. Hudson did not like the poems. Davies mistook them for Frost's work, and others suggested he re-write sections of them. He resisted.

It seems likely that Thomas might have gone in one of two directions early in 1915. One possibility was to return with Frost to America together with Merfyn; the other, to enlist. Something however occurred on New Year's Day which fortuitously put both options out of the question, and directly affected the flood of work that was by now pouring from him. Coming down the steep hillside above his Hampshire village on his way home , he fell awkwardly and sprained his ankle badly. For a week he was confined to bed, and for another seven or so weeks, he was required to walk with care. There was nothing to do but write poetry, and in just two days, between 7 January and 9 January, five more were created, including that memory of a June train journey to Dymock, 'Adlestrop'. He was also working on a patriotic anthology of English writers called appropriately *This England*, "as simple and rich as a plum pudding". When the book came out, of all the friends only Abercrombie recognised two poems by 'Edward Eastaway', namely 'Haymaking' and 'The Manor Farm', although another to see through the literary disguise early was John Haines. Thus these become the first poems by Edward Thomas to appear in print. The only other contemporary poets represented in the book are Hardy, Bottomley, and de la Mare. "I wished," wrote Thomas in the Preface, "to make a book as full of English character and country as an egg is of meat". But above all it was the poetry that was important now. After the earlier rejections the tide began to turn; James Guthrie accepted two for a 1915 edition of his quarterly journal, *Root and Branch*, and the following year placed two more in another magazine, *Form*.

On 11 February Helen left Steep with Merfyn, who was bound for Liverpool and America with the Frosts. Thomas was by this time able to walk, but not far, and so was unable to accompany them. The original plan had been for Thomas himself to bring Merfyn to Little Iddens, spending a last night with the Frosts before they all left together the next day for Liverpool. The sprain had put paid to this plan, and it was a simpler journey for Helen to go direct to Liverpool and meet the Americans there. So Edward said goodbye to his son in the doorway of Yew Tree Cottage in Steep. The relationship between Merfyn and his father was always a complex and sometimes very difficult one, and the poem that came out of this event, 'Parting', says much about Thomas's sense of regret:

> ...memory made
> Parting today a double pain:
> First because it was parting; next
> Because the ill it ended vexed
> And mocked me from the Past again...

On 28 February, two weeks after the Frosts sailed, Rupert Brooke had just recovered from a bad cold which took a long time to get over and was embarking at Bristol on the *Grantully Castle*, a seven-thousand ton Union Castle liner, converted as a troop ship. His recent illness had affected him more severely than he might have expected, leaving him debilitated and rather depressed. Added to which, the loss of increasing numbers of his comrades, and friends from Rugby and Cambridge, lowered his spirits. James Elroy Flecker had just died of tuberculosis in Switzerland. Brooke wrote his obituary for *The Times*. Just a week before embarkation he and his men had been told at Blandford that they were to be sent to take Constantinople and break through into the Black Sea. It was secretly believed that heavy casualties could be expected, and that his Hood battalion would be in the forefront of the action. It is uncertain as to whether Brooke ever saw the last edition of *New Numbers* containing his war sonnets, other than in proof form. Nor can I find evidence to support the fact that Brooke returned to Dymock once more, which makes a reminiscence by Catherine Abercrombie rather puzzling. In her 1956 radio talk she says:

> I remember him [Rupert] so well when he came to say "good-bye" before going off on the disastrous Gallipoli expedition. There was a huge sloping field of scarlet poppies coming down to the edge of our garden. I can see him now standing gazing absorbedly at them and saying to me "I shall always

remember that — always." He had never really got over the
Antwerp failure, when such a lot of men came back ill with
dysentery, and he was not really well enough to start off again;
but he was so keen to throw himself into the thick of things,
and tried to tease my husband into joining him. [TL 15 January
1956 p.794]

As Brooke sailed in February, it seems likely that the "poppy field"
reference dates from the previous summer, when Brooke was at
Dymock on at least two occasions. The occasion of the poppies was
also picked up by Gibson, who wrote it into his four-part elegy
'Rupert Brooke':

> Your eyes rejoiced in colour's ecstasy,
> Fulfilling even their uttermost desire,
> When, over a great sunlit field afire
> With windy poppies streaming like a sea
> Of scarlet flame that flaunted riotously
> Among green orchards of that western shire,
> You gazed as though your heart could never tire
> Of life's red flood in summer revelry...

For the rest it is probably a composite memory, the sort of trick that
time can play. Certainly it is a fact that Brooke had egged on Abercrombie much as he had done Drinkwater. Indeed, one of his last
letters from the *Grantully Castle*, off Egypt on 6 April, is written to
Abercrombie. During the early part of the month, Brooke suffered
badly from heatstroke and dysentery. These attacks weakened him
critically, shortly leading to his death. Nevertheless, even at this late
stage, the teasing referred to by Catherine is present in the letter:

> I wonder if you're an A.S.C. train officer, or a Lowell lecturer,
> by now. Have your plans matured, at all? Has Eddie pushed
> you into one of the various R.N.D. transport vacancies created
> by our removal in this crusade? It would be fun if one could
> think you were coming out in a future batch — in time to
> reverse 1453, and celebrate mass in St. Sophia. [RB/GK p .678]

The letter ends with a final "come and join us", and a request after
the Gibsons' health. What also becomes clear from this letter, and
from Brooke's earlier one to Drinkwater, is that at this stage the
Dymock brotherhood had decided to discontinue *New Numbers*. It

has been suggested that the idea came after Brooke's death, as a mark of respect. In fact, probably because of declining subscriptions during the war, but also because of war shortages generally, it had already been planned that issue four would be the last. Earlier Brooke had suggested to Drinkwater from Blandford that there might be a way he could devise to pick him and Gibson and Abercrombie up from Dymock, and "bury *New Numbers* with a Resurgam". Although he does not comment on seeing the last issue personally, he has read a review in *The Times* "by a laudatory half-wit", who seems to have missed the fact that this was the last issue, and Brooke suggested that perhaps they should have inserted a slip to make the point, "and extracted, even in these times, a few tears, a few shillings".

And so the little Georgian magazine that had sent the name of Dymock all over the world met its end, shortly before one of its most distinguishing lights also went out forever. Rupert Brooke died of blood poisoning at 4.46 p.m. on 23 April 1915. This young man, so much the personification of an idealised English patriotism and an undoubted star in the Georgian firmament, breathed his last on, of all days, St George's Day, Shakespeare's presumed birth and deathday, and the sixty-fifth anniversary of the death of William Wordsworth. He was buried on the Greek island of Skyros, and his companions sailed for Gallipoli. Edward Thomas wrote to Robert Frost that "All the papers are full of his 'beauty', and an eloquent last sonnet beginning 'If I should die'. He was eloquent. Men never spoke ill of him... I should like another April week in Gloucestershire with you like the one last year. You are the only person I can be idle with. That's natural history, not eloquence".

The papers were indeed full of Rupert Brooke. Churchill wrote a letter to *The Times*, drawing attention to "the incomparable war sonnets". In the same paper was Marsh's short unsigned obituary. Dean Inge read 'The Soldier' from the pulpit of St Paul's Cathedral. Demand for Issue Four of *New Numbers* exceeded all possibility of keeping pace. To many, it seemed almost as though it had been written in some tragic play. D.H. Lawrence wrote: "He was slain by bright Phoebus' shaft... it was the real climax of his pose... Bright Phoebus smote him down. It is all in the saga. O God, O God, it is all too much of a piece: it is like madness". Gibson's reaction, shy and overawed by Brooke, was deeply personal: "When I was with him I used to wonder and wonder — is it possible that this radiant creature can really care for me? I always thought of him as one of the Sons of the Morning". Care Brooke most certainly did, to the extent that he had named Gibson and Abercrombie, together with de la Mare, as the beneficiaries of his royalties. He had written his reason thus: "If I can set them free, to any extent, to write the poetry and plays and books they want to, my death will bring more gain than loss". After his affairs had been put in order, each received £166.19s.8d. However, this was only the start. Brooke was about to be canonised in the public esteem, and his bequest, given the huge sales of his books for the next twenty years, was to prove a thing that was to make Abercrombie and Gibson secure for the rest of their lives. Both men joined in the deluge of elegiac poems — of all qualities — dedicated to the memory of Brooke. Gibson wrote at least three poems in an outpouring of grief for his friend. Abercrombie picked up the image of both Lawrence and Gibson in his:

> All things were turned to fire in him, and cast
> The light of their transfiguring round his ways,
> His secret gleamed upon us; where he past
> He shone; he brought with him a golden place.

On 16 June a posthumous volume of Brooke's work *1914 and Other Poems* was published. The book contained the famous sonnets, but also the 'South Sea' poems, bringing to a wider public most of the poems that had originally appeared in *New Numbers* and causing the *New Statesman* critic to comment, "A myth has been created: but it has grown round an imaginary figure very different from the real man... Some of the Deans and great-aunts who picture Brooke as a kind of blend of General Gordon and Lord Tennyson will have a jolt when they read the poem on the theology of fishes".

On 17 July Brooke's effects arrived in packages at Marsh's apartment. He took them straight away to Rugby, and handed them over to Mrs Brooke, who seemed at first to be composed in her grief, but when she opened the packages she at last gave way to her sorrow, and "I have never seen such suffering," wrote Marsh to Henry James, "It was very terrible". Marsh himself was still in a state of high emotion. After his stay with Brooke's mother, he went straight to Dymock, where he stayed for the next eight days. Asking the Gibsons to give him a quiet room in which he could work, he shut himself away entirely for the whole of that time, and worked on his

Memoir of his friend, finishing it at 2.00 a.m. on Tuesday 27 July. In it he spoke of Brooke's development as a poet, and of his methods of composition, including the *New Numbers* project: "They meant at first to call it *The Gallows Garland*, after The Gallows, Abercrombie's cottage in Gloucestershire, from which it was to be published; and Rupert thought the change very stupid". Marsh's slim *Memoir* was a labour of love in which he tried to "draw him as I see him"; having passed it to Mrs Brooke to read, it became clear however that she would not allow publication of the work in its current form. "It doesn't represent Rupert as he really was at all," she complained, "It must be completely reworked." The *Memoir* was to go through four more drafts before agreement between Mrs Brooke and Marsh came to pass, and the work took its place, greatly enlarged by much new material, at the head of the amazingly successful *Collected Poems* published in 1918.

*

When the Frosts arrived in America, a problem developed over the 15-year-old Merfyn Thomas's papers, and he was retained for a time on Ellis Island, a testing time which saw Frost in one of his rages before finally things were smoothed out, and the boy was put on a train to Alstead, New Hampshire where he was to stay with Russell Scott, a relative of his father's. Thomas himself, once he began to find his feet again, was far from idle, working on the "filthy job" of the seventy-five thousand word biography of Marlborough which was to occupy him until the beginning of June. The effect was to dry up — temporarily — the stream of poems that had been so prolific. Nevertheless in April he sent a copy of 'Lob' to Frost, producing the response: "You are a poet or you are nothing". In spite of other intrusions on his writing time, and the necessity of accepting the Marlborough commission, 'Lob' was Thomas's fifty-sixth poem since the beginning of December. By the end of the year the total was to rise to ninety-three. Frost's April letter also takes the opportunity of deriding Gibson, who had written to him to announce that he had made contact with Ellery Sedgwick of the *Atlantic* and "rather invited himself over". Frost's view of things was that Gibson had asked Sedgwick to arrange a reading tour for him. Gibson on the other hand was claiming, according to Frost, that "he had been urged to come over and save the country". Clearly his disillusionment with the Hexham man still ran deep. In the same month, John Haines had a letter from the American, deeply concerned about the war, and missing his English friends.

As the year progressed Thomas's ankle healed and he was able to start travelling again. He stayed with Haines and showed him his poems, talking with him about the drudgery of writing *Marlborough* and jokingly regretted that it was about the Duke and not the town. When the book was at last finished, Thomas wrote an article on Brooke for the June edition of the *English Review*. "No poet of his age," he wrote, "was so much esteemed and admired, or was watched more hopefully. His work could not be taken soberly, whether you liked it or not". Not another Shelley, judged Thomas, although fired by much the same poetic hope and "perhaps no poet better expressed the aspiration towards it and all the unfulfilled eagerness of ambitious self-conscious youth". This work done, Thomas's desk had cleared, and it would seem that it was with some relief and in need of spiritual refreshment that he turned back again to *North of Boston*. Frost's poems acted like a charge to tired batteries, a forceful renewing of purpose in his own writing. Perhaps spurred by this, and overcome with a sudden desire to be back in the Gloucestershire countryside of their companionship, he set off in June to spend three days with Haines. In a letter to Frost he says that the American was very much a part of their conversation as they sat or cycled the lanes again. Haines remembered how they "walked or bicycled over Birdlip Hill to the old Cotswold town of Painswick, through the Forest of Dean to Symonds Yat...he taking the keenest interest in every sight and sound and smell". Thomas was taking stock of himself before the next decisive moment which was fast approaching. Significantly Haines and Thomas went to May Hill, "whence," as Haines recalled, "sitting down, he could see the hills of Wales, 'And Herefordshire,/ And the villages there' as he wrote. He brought it down written out to breakfast next morning, and finally polished it on the road to Coventry in the afternoon...":

> Out of us all
> That make rhymes,
> Will you choose
> Sometimes —
> As the winds use
> A crack in a wall
> Or a drain,
> Their joy or their pain

To whistle through —
Choose me,
You English words?

Even up to the first week of July Thomas was still considering which
direction to take; he wrote to Frost that he still thought about the
American option. Then he changed his mind again; on Wednesday
14 July, he enlisted with the Artists' Rifles, and by the beginning of
the following week, billetted with his parents, he had begun training
in London.

10. Dear Boys,
They've Killed Our Woods

> I have lived in Gloucestershire, and I have known what it is
> to have Wilfrid Gibson and Robert Frost for my neighbours;
> and John Drinkwater, Rupert Brooke, Edward Thomas, Will
> Davies, Bob Trevelyan, Arthur Ransome have drunk my cider
> and talkt [sic] in my garden. I make no cider now, and I have
> no garden. But once I lived in Gloucestershire. [JG pp.20-21]

Such was Lascelles Abercrombie's sad epilogue to his glorious
Dymock years, in a collection of autobiographical essays gathered
by John Gawsworth towards the end of Abercrombie's life. The
whole thing had happened so quickly, had been so concentrated in
its essence, rather like good cider; perhaps also like good cider, it had
been rather too strong to last, or to consume in too great a quantity.
In well under a decade, the Dymock poets as a group came and went.
Beyond Dymock life and death went on, and rather like a tide
working on a headland, gradually and inexorably broke up the last
stranded elements of the group, although at first, as with all forms
of evolution, it looked more like change than an ending.

In September 1915 Robert Frost wrote a long, almost one might call
it, a homesick letter to Lascelles Abercrombie. In it he looks back on
Ryton and the Dymock circle as on an already distant and golden
time. Perhaps it was because of his own situation in America, starting
to improve but still financially fragile, and with Elinor enduring a
new and troublesome seventh pregnancy, accompanied by an illness
which seemed to be more serious. The pregnancy ended with a
miscarriage in November. Frost remembered that Abercrombie's
review of *North of Boston* had been his first favourable review, and

137

"there will never be any other like it". Intriguingly he adds that he would be happy to join with Abercrombie "in your next enterprise if you will have me". Whether this implies that there was an attempt at bringing a Dymock circle back together it is difficult to say. Whatever it was, it appears to have come to nothing. Frost ends, "Now I should like to go out into the yard and shake hands with your big cold pump till his iron tank was as full of water as my heart is of Ryton memories". Frost adds a postscript, a note about Edward Thomas. He feels, he says, that the war has made "some sort of new man and a poet" out of him.

Meanwhile in the autumn of 1915, John Drinkwater directed the first performance of Gordon Bottomley's controversial Georgian play, *King Lear's Wife*. This took the realism of the Georgians to new heights — many critics said depths; critics were savage, calling it "a beastly play" and "a tragedy that prostitutes art". Almost at the same time the second Georgian anthology — postponed from the previous year — appeared. *Georgian Poetry 1913-1915* was published in October of the year. It ultimately exceeded the sales of volume one, but it was in a way an anachronism; postponed from the previous year, it took little account of the fact that the world had changed a lot in the intervening months. It was mainly the same book as would have appeared earlier, with one or two exceptions. Bottomley's play shared some of the attacks with Abercrombie's 'End of the World' in the same volume, printed again after its appearance in *New Numbers*. It was a dark time in the war, the Defence of the Realm Act was in force, there was a reaction now against the "over by Christmas" mood of the previous autumn. Now things seemed to be going nowhere. Yet in this new book, with the exception of four poems, the war was ignored almost totally. These four poems were a tribute to Brooke by Gibson, Brooke's own 'The Soldier', Drinkwater's 'Of Greatham' and a poem by the late James Elroy Flecker, 'The Dying Patriot'. Georgian volumes were to continue to be published at regular intervals until 1922, by which time the claim of the first volume, that it heralded some sort of renaissance, had become a cause for sardonic mirth among the emerging Modernists.

The year 1915 gave way to 1916 and Drinkwater's *The Storm*, first published in *New Numbers 3*, and by now a guaranteed success whenever it was staged, was revived at Birmingham. Then came another verse play from his prolific pen, *The God of Quiet*, described as "a parable of war and peace" taking place on a hill outside a besieged city. The play was written in rhyming verse, and, catching the mood of the time, appealed to audiences at 'The Rep'. In December he wrote the Birmingham pantomime *Puss in Boots*. In the same year, a new era began for Drinkwater when he met the artist William Rothenstein, who was at the time establishing his recently restored seventeenth century farmhouse Iles Farm at Far Oakridge as a spiritual hub for artists and writers alike. Just north of the main Stroud to Cirencester Road, it was and is an area of great Cotswold beauty, and Drinkwater loved it. Ultimately he was to move there towards the end of the war, to a cottage previously lived in by Max Beerbohm. It was while here that Drinkwater wrote what was probably his most popular play, *Abraham Lincoln*. The work was first performed and published in 1918, and Barry Jackson was to claim that it was one of only two plays that had paid for itself in the early life of The Rep. Within its first year *Abraham Lincoln* went through eight impressions with the publishers Sidgwick and Jackson, and was still bringing in audiences in Station Street into the 1950s.

It was also from Far Oakridge, in 1917, that Drinkwater published his *Prose Papers*, containing his essay on Rupert Brooke, mentioned earlier. Apart from the Brooke essay, he writes on a wide variety of subjects, including the nature of drama, art, poetry in education and a number of poets, among them Chaucer, Gray, Coleridge, Sidney and the Brontes. Many of these pieces were digested from reviews, as with his article on Rupert Brooke's (now published) Cambridge dissertation study of John Webster, in which Drinkwater anticipates Marsh's *Memoir*, at this time still the subject of discussion between Marsh and Mrs Brooke. The book of essays is dedicated to William Rothenstein, "in homage" to his work as an artist, whose work "the contemplation of which is a daily and growing inspiration to my own life and work. Then it is to thank you for having found me a corner of your enchanted Cotswold country".

Drinkwater had indeed found a new circle, but he was not to forget the past, and the dedication includes a vivid little character sketch of the Dymock years, and some of the powerful personalities who were involved in the group:

> With many of the Georgian Poets, my collaborators in *New Numbers* and others, I have formed close friendships, and I know of nothing more splendid than the way in which these men, with various and often violently opposing views about

> their art, realise that they are working for a common end, and
> are enthusiastic one for another's success — allowing always,
> of course, a resentment of dishonest work. [PP p.5]

Drinkwater left Gloucestershire in 1921, divorced and remarried. In 1928 he published his study of Charles James Fox, a large-scale work in which he examined minutely the life and work of "perhaps the greatest figure in the history of Parliamentary opposition in England". He died in 1937, at the age of only fifty-five.

*

In December 1915 Merfyn Thomas came home from America. The previous month his father's book on the Duke of Marlborough had been published. Thomas was moving towards publication of the poems more confidently, and in March 1916 sent forty poems to Gordon Bottomley. Bottomley, Abercrombie and R.C. Trevelyan were discussing possible contents of a new anthology to be published by Constable in 1917 as *An Annual of New Poetry*. When the book eventually appeared, it contained no less than eighteen poems by 'Edward Eastaway'. It was also fitting that there should be some of Frost's work there too, and Wilfrid Gibson's. In June 1916 Thomas was awarded a £300 grant instead of a Civil List Pension, and in the same month he applied for a commission in the artillery, (he was to be commissioned as a second lieutenant in November). Much of the intervening time was given over to training, first in London, and then in Wiltshire during October. This gave him the opportunity of visiting Haines in Gloucester, and the two men walked in Cranham Woods, "famous even in the Cotswolds", writes Haines, "for their magnificent autumn colouring". Haines also remembered that Thomas was more talkative than usual on this occasion, discussing Blake, Shelley and Spenser, while sitting on a fallen tree "where he could see the plants of Deadly Nightshade for which he had set me to search... Later, still sitting on the tree trunk, he became quite excited in describing his favourite combinations of colour, in tree and leaf, berry and flower — the feathers of Traveller's Joy mixed with Hawthorn or Briony berries and crimson Blackberry leaves and so on...". Perhaps coincidentally it was this same month that saw publication of *The Flowers I Love*, an anthology compiled by Thomas with colour drawings by Katherine Cameron. Also in October he was checking the proofs of the eighteen 'Eastaway' poems that were to appear in *An Annual of New Poetry*. Among them were some of his early work, including 'Old Man', and another later poem about his youngest daughter, 'The Brook', written shortly before he had enlisted. One of Frost's favourite poems, 'Aspens', was there ("Aspens...seems the loveliest of all" — Frost). But there was also work that reflected his present situation, 'A Private', and a poem that seemed somehow to encapsulate his past and future, 'Roads':

> Now all roads lead to France
> And heavy is the tread
> Of the living; but the dead
> Returning lightly dance...

He was working to meet Frost's exhortation to prepare a complete collection "for when you come marching home". In December he volunteered for overseas service, and on 29 January 1917 he embarked for France. Just a week earlier he had come to Gloucestershire for what was to be one final visit, meeting Haines on 22 January, and staying until the following afternoon. Haines remembered him as being more cheerful than he had seen him before, and certainly more healthy in physical appearance than he had seemed on the autumn visit. "He appeared to be glad to be done with waiting," Haines recalled. Perhaps it was because at last he could see himself being judged by simple standards. As Thomas wrote to Bottomley of his situation at this time, "I can only fail because I couldn't succeed". Or perhaps it was because he knew he could be both a poet and a soldier. A collection was, as Frost had hoped, now on the way, and "will probably be published while I am out". Yet Haines felt a overwhelming premonition that he would not come back, "and that he knew it". He studied Haines's poetry library, casting opinions of all kinds as he browsed along the shelves, settling finally on the latest volume of poems by Robert Frost, *Mountain Interval*. The book had been published during 1916, and as we have seen, contained much implicit imagery of the Dymock months, including 'The Road Not Taken', and 'The Cow in Apple Time': "Her face is flecked with pomace and she drools/A cider syrup". Perhaps it was no surprise to Haines when Thomas asked him if he could take the book with him to France. Certainly he made no objection: "I saw him off by train next day, and he sailed for France a few days later. He was the most loveable man that ever lived — that is all".

THE DYMOCK POETS

Shortly after Edward's departure for France, Frost wrote an excited letter to Helen to tell her that he had found an American publisher for Thomas's poetry. By the last week in March the news had reached Edward, who wrote to Bottomley that he still wanted to maintain his anonymity. In the same letter Thomas comments with concern on the continuing writers' block the war had created in Abercrombie. He is also now anxious to see the *Annual of New Poetry*, just published by Constable. The letter arrived with Bottomley on 27 March, and the next day he replied, telling Thomas that Trevelyan had sent his copy of the *Annual* to Loughton instead of direct to France, but that hopefully it would arrive soon. There were as yet no reviews available, but Bottomley enclosed a 'Books Received' notice from the *Times Literary Supplement*. He also reported that Gibson was still on his reading tour of America and was "having a good deal of success". The full review from the *Times Literary Supplement* of 29 March 1917 on the *Annual* arrived with Thomas in the same post as Bottomley's letter. In it, the reviewer commented on Thomas: "At present, like most of his contemporaries, he has too little control over his eyes... Or is the new method an unconscious survival of a materialism and naturalism which the tremendous life of the last three years has made an absurdity...". The irony was not lost on Thomas, in the thick of things at the front, near Arras: "Must I see only Huns in these beautiful hills...?". But he would have been pleased with one line in the critic's notice, a line that stated everything that needed to be said: "He is a real poet, with the truth in him". When Thomas replied, he gave Bottomley a graphic picture of his situation, "muddy to the waist", but the closing paragraphs show a shared feeling for Abercrombie's predicament, with Thomas hoping "to see him and new work of his some day. I do not know his equal for keenness and warmth". By coincidence, the Army Service Corps driver attached to Thomas's unit came from a corner of England close to "where I last saw Frost and Abercrombie, and it was a pleasure to talk about those villages...". Thomas wrote this in his letter on 4 April. Five days later, on 9 April — Easter Monday — he was killed by blast from a shell that passed close to his observation post. He left one hundred and forty-four poems, written in just over two years.

After Thomas's death, there were several attempts by many of his contemporaries, including Gibson and Abercrombie, to persuade Edward Marsh to admit him to the *Georgian Poetry* anthologies.

Freeman, Turner and de la Mare were even prepared to forego their place in the book to make way for him. Freeman was outspoken in his insistence:

> I've had the privilege of seeing probably the whole of his verse...so far as my own opinion might stretch or be worth anything it would be splendid if the next G.P. book included any other new poetry of comparable individuality and power. [MLC, Berg Collection]

Marsh steadfastly refused, on the ostensible grounds that this was to be a collection of living writers, and no one should be represented posthumously, a curious decision, given the war and its toll. It would seem that there was something rather more deep-seated than this, perhaps dating back to the unfortunate encounter when Brooke had brought Thomas to breakfast at Gray's Inn in February 1913. Certainly there would seem to have been an entrenched opinion behind a remark in a letter to Marsh from Robert Graves, early in 1918:

> I have a new poet for you, just discovered, one Wilfred Owen: this is a real find, not a sudden lo here! or lo there! which unearths an Edward Eastaway or a Vernede, but the real thing... [EM/CH p.437]

*

During the busy months leading up to Edward Thomas's final embarkation, Haines had sent him some news which, in less hectic times, would have saddened him. "We wrote telling him of the destruction of some of the beautiful trees near Abercrombie's cottage" Haines said, but Thomas felt he would only regret their loss when the war was over, "if I regret anything then". For Abercrombie, it must have seemed a cruel metaphor, framing his happy Dymock years with the burst of daffodils that had greeted his arrival. The opening words of one of his best poems, dedicated to his three sons David, Michael and Ralph, are eloquent:

> Dear boys, they've killed our woods: the ground
> Now looks ashamed, to be shorn so bare;
> Naked lank ridge and brooding mound
> Seem shivering cowed in the April air.
> They well may starve, hills that have been
> So richly and so sturdily fleeced!

THE DYMOCK POETS

Who made this upland, once so green,
Crouch comfortless, like an ill-used beast?

There was a fool who had pulled fierce faces
At his photographer thirty years;
He swore, Now I'll put you through your paces,
Jaegers, Uhlans, and Grenadiers!

Was he to blame? Or the looking-glass
That taught him his moustachioes?
How could that joke for an Attila pass?
Who was to blame? Nobody knows.

Of all the poets Abercrombie seems to have been most adversely affected by the war in terms of poetic output. He became depressed and unable to write. Several times he had attempted to enlist, but was each time turned down on medical grounds. In the end, desperate to help in some way, in April 1916 he volunteered to work at steel-testing at a huge ammunition works near Liverpool. He would return to Ryton as often as he could, but in the meantime he was looking for a new home for Catherine and the three boys. On one occasion while Lascelles was in Liverpool, a poignant incident occurred while Catherine was playing with her children in a field near The Gallows. "A youth in khaki came walking towards us, asking if I could direct him to Lascelles Abercrombie's cottage, as he wanted to see it, and him, if possible." The young soldier was the poet and composer Ivor Gurney, and Catherine befriended him, taking him home to tea, and afterwards keeping in touch for a while, sending out literary papers and news to him at the front, although "after a time we lost touch with him and found he had been put into an asylum as his mind had been badly affected...". In due course Lascelles found a house near his work, and "we broke up our home and went to live in Liverpool".

In Bottomley's last letter to Edward Thomas, there is some clue as to Abercrombie's predicament. In it he speaks of Lascelles' inability to write, and of his frustration at being rejected for the army. Apparently he "had a definite intention of joining George Trevelyan in Italy and working in a mountain ambulance". But in addition to all his other problems, Catherine became ill, and he would not go far afield until he knew she was safe. Bottomley goes on:

The weary round of ugliness and repetition in an engineer's shop or any kind of works or office is worse to bear than anything else for someone with such creative energy and vision as his and (at a guess) I fancy he felt it a hateful and hope-destroying slavery. [ET/GB p.282]

After the war Abercrombie turned to the academic life, teaching at various universities and writing a number of well-respected treatises on aspects of literature. In 1919 he became a lecturer in poetry studies at Liverpool University, moving from there in 1922 to Leeds, where he was Professor of English. In 1923 Trinity College, Cambridge invited him as Clark Lecturer and the subject matter, modified by a subsequent Ballard Matthews Lecture Series in the University College of North Wales, formed the basis of a book published in 1925 by Secker under the title *The Idea of Great Poetry*. Of this book one critic eulogised: "Nobody who cares for great poetry should miss this book," and while criticising "Mr Abercrombie's occasional tendency to long-winded and long-worded discussions on the abstract", applauds Abercrombie for insisting that "in poetry...the supreme greatness demands scale". It was a rearguard action by Abercrombie against the encroaching forces of Modernism, defending, as he saw it, "Form — coherence — unity — these are well-worn terms; and just because they are, I thought it a fitting topic for such a course as this to argue in favour of their unchangeable importance...". Remembering John Haines's impression of him as a forceful and beautiful speaker, we may feel confident that he was equal to his case before his audience.

In 1928, while Abercrombie was at Leeds, and by now a chronic diabetic, the past was brought flooding back by a visit to England from Robert Frost. It must have been a difficult occasion for both men; Frost's star was now rising, and there seemed little common ground between the two men, with Abercrombie sick and disillusioned. In spite of his academic successes he was still a frustrated gipsy. Gibson too was far from the old scenes, living in Letchworth. Frost was undecided about a visit to him, after the awkwardness between the two men. But there was further acrimony when he visited Helen Thomas, who had not long before published a very personal memoir of her life with Edward. Frost could not forgive her for in his view sanitizing Edward's memory, and the difference caused a permanent rift between the two. A reading at the Poetry

Bookshop had been arranged for the American, and, although he had not contacted Gibson, word of the appearance reached his former friend's current home at Letchworth, and Wilfrid wrote a warm letter:

> I have just received a Poetry Bookshop announcement which says that Robert Frost is reading his poems there on the 18th... We are thrilled to think that there may be a chance of seeing you again, at last! Even though you never answer letters, you do remember us, don't you, and those old days in Gloucester-shire. I cannot tell you with what warm affection we always think of you and yours. [RF/LT/YT p.335]

So a visit to Letchworth was arranged during October, and it was an easy occasion, with the Gibsons plying the Frosts with happy recol-lections, and no unpleasant questions. Afterwards, the now out-of-favour Gibson sent Frost, in his habitual manner, a poem about the meeting in which, as Frost later told Haines, "he stoutly excuses us all for looking so horribly old". The poem appeared in Gibson's next book, published in 1930, called *Hazards*:

> Disastrous years have had their way with us:
> Terrors and desolations and distresses,
> That put a sudden period to our youth
> Just when our powers were ripening, left us aged
> Before our time...

Of all his late-twenties English friends, Frost now perhaps had more in common with Haines; at least with him he could tramp the old Dymock lanes again, and remember the old times with someone who in a sense still lived them in his mind. They climbed May Hill as a tribute to Edward Thomas and, as Haines remembered, "the wraith of that dead friend was ever before us...". Nearly thirty years later, Frost would chase the same ghost over the same ground.

*

If we look for Dymock and its area in the poems, literally translated as place into words, we are most likely to find it in the works of Wilfrid Gibson. He was, as we have seen, the 'chronicler' of the group, and many of his poems are direct pictures of the rural life he saw around him at the Greenway. In Bottomley's *An Annual of New*

Poetry at least four of the six poems by which he is represented may be seen to have Gloucestershire themes, 'The Platelayer', 'In the Meadow', 'The Plough', and, explicitly, 'Daffodils', set as it is:

> ...beneath the Malvern hills,
> A little fellow plucking daffodils,
> ....In his blue frock among that laughing yellow,
> And plovers in their sheeny black and white
> Flirting and tumbling in the morning light
> About his curly head. He still could see,
> Shutting his eyes, as plain as plain could be,
> Drift upon drift, those long-dead daffodils
> Against the far green of the Malvern hills,
> Nodding and laughing round his little lad,
> As if to see him happy made them glad —
> Nodding and laughing...

Likewise in the four sonnets collectively entitled 'Home' he speaks specifically of "the brown bird-haunted eaves of thatch", and "the midnight pillars of black elms...". In his war-time poem 'The Ragged Stone', he uses a local legend to reflect contemporary trauma. The poem tells the tale of a young soldier upon whom the shadow of "The Ragged Stone" falls, and the fears of his lover for his safety. Ragged Stone Hill, an outcrop of the Malverns, is not far from The Greenway. Gibson may well have known the ancient story of an ownership dispute between monks from Little Malvern and the Lord of the Manor of Birtsmorton. One day this lord, so the story goes, found a monk on Ragged Stone Hill, and told him to go. The monk refused, and prophesied that whenever the shadow of the stone outcrop on the hill fell on the lord's home below, within twelve months the death would occur of the eldest son of the family. Roy Palmer in his book *The Folklore of Hereford and Worcester* points out that the sun can only thus fall on a certain day in November. According to the story, the family of the officious lord died out in impoverished circumstances in Worcester during the nineteenth century. But there is another version, with which Gibson may have been more familiar. In 1888 Charles F. Grindrod published a novel, *The Shadow of the Ragged Stone*. Here a monk from the same priory defies his vow of chastity and strikes up a liaison with a local woman. His penance, when his sin is discovered, is to crawl up the hill to the Ragged Stone. With his dying breath he issues a curse upon whom-

soever the shadow of the Ragged Stone should fall. One or both of
these stories may have influenced Gibson to write his poem, but the
spirit of the piece is undoubtedly that of First World War Britain:

> As I was walking with my dear, my dear come back at last,
> The shadow of the Ragged Stone fell on us as we passed:
>
> And if the tale be true they tell about the Ragged Stone,
> I'll not be walking with my dear next year, nor yet alone.
>
> And we're to wed come Michaelmas, my lovely dear and I;
> And we're to have a little house, and do not want to die.
>
> But all the folk are fighting in the lands across the sea
> Because the king and counsellors went mad in Germany.
>
> Because the king and counsellors went mad, my love and I
> May never have a little house before we come to die:
>
> And if the tale be true they tell about the Ragged Stone,
> I'll not be walking with my dear next year, nor yet alone.

In spite of numerous attempts at enlisting, Gibson's generally
fragile health and poor eyesight kept him out of the military conflict
for the first part of the war. He was medically B II, and appears to
have suffered from illnesses perhaps stemming from dietary inade-
quacies. In March 1916, a month before Abercrombie left for Liverpool, he had to have his appendix removed. As he recuperated, he
would have noted the melancholy fact of Abercrombie's departure, and
that he was now the only poet of the brotherhood left in Dymock. In
October 1916 he and Geraldine, together with their new baby, moved
away themselves, to West Malvern, at which time he commented
that the climate at Greenway had "never suited any of us". He
succeeded in arranging his reading tour of the United States, where
his reputation as a poet was still high. Between 23 December 1916
and late July 1917 he read in cities between New York and Chicago.
The tour was highly successful, although Gibson's wilful disregard
of all things technical seems to have taken some of the learned
academics he met rather aback; notably at the University of Chicago,
where he proudly boasted that he was "not very familiar with metre
and versification". It was during this part of his tour, while he was
staying with a Mrs William Vaughn Moody, that Gibson had an

awkward encounter with Frost. His hostess, unaware of the tension between the two men, had invited the American to stay, and just before he left, welcomed Gibson. Frost wrote to her making his feelings plain: "Enter distinguished Englishman, exit extinguished American".

After his return from the American tour, Gibson was at last successful in his attempts at joining up. Up until this time his health and eyesight had been grounds enough to keep him out of the services, but by 1917 the war was consuming men too fast for the authorities to have much choice, and he was accepted into the Army Service Corps, becoming Private Gibson T/38190. Shortly after his enlistment, Haines met him in his private's uniform on a platform at Paddington Station, although he did not recognise him at first. It was very late at night, and Gibson was distraught. He told Haines that he had just heard that Geraldine had fallen downstairs, and was severely injured. The authorities had given him compassionate leave, but had not allowed him to go until this time, by now too late to catch a train home to Malvern, where she was in hospital. "He was in a dreadful state of mind," Haines later recalled. Fortunately Geraldine recovered.

Gibson's work involved him in general clerical duties, as well as work loading lorries, a task for which he hardly seems to have been suited. He loathed the experience, and received his discharge papers with immense relief. Nevertheless his final report praises him as an "efficient and reliable clerk". While in the army Gibson continued to write poems of ordinary life, but this time he transferred the action to the grim reality of the things he saw in the course of his duties. They are poems which reflect a very different world to the early heroics; at last Georgian realism had subject matter to more than match its ethic, and in these poems Gibson is concerned to show how cheap life has become, and how thin are the lines between normality and oblivion. He paints a picture of soldiers who eat on their backs because of the shells, and who endure appalling conditions while retaining humour and home values. In 'Elegy' he writes of Man as a light: "For a little while he burns/Fitfully...". This sensitive man was deeply affected by the loss, and perhaps felt that any attempt at return to the idyll as it had been before the war was unthinkable. This certainly is the mood of his poem, 'Lament':

...A bird in the rain-wet lilac sings

But we — how shall we turn to little things
And listen to the birds and winds and streams
Made holy by their dreams,
Nor feel the heart-break in the heart of things?

After the war Gibson spent much time on lecture and reading tours around Britain, keeping up a punishing schedule, and continuing to write his poems as prolifically as ever. In 1925 Macmillan published his *Collected Poems*, but from then on his work seems to have gone out of favour. Nevertheless the readings continued until the outbreak of the Second World War, when he was over sixty. Then hostilities put an end to such activities.

One of Gibson's faults, as Edward Thomas identified, was that he simply wrote too much too uncritically. Another, was that he consciously went out and looked for his poems, rather than allowing them to come to him. This is graphically demonstrated in a recollection of Frost's. On the occasion in question, the two men had been coming home from a point-to-point meeting, when Gibson turned to Frost and said uneasily, "I didn't see a thing there I could use, did you?". As he grew older, he seems to have been concerned about his financial welfare, although the benefits he continued to receive from Brooke's estate must have considerably eased the burden of the effect of his declining popularity on his book sales. Yet he continued to pour out his prolific although uneven work, producing a further twelve volumes between 1926 and 1950, when his last collection, *Within Four Walls*, was published. In that year Geraldine died. He lingered on for a further twelve years, writing no more. Then in May 1962, in a nursing home at Virginia Water, he died at the age of eighty-four. The shadows cast by 'The Golden Room' fell over his whole life, as he recalled with nostalgia the brief moment when it had all seemed to come together at The Old Nailshop, Greenway, only to burst like a coloured bubble:

Now, on the crest of an Aegean isle,
Brooke sleeps, and dreams of England: Thomas lies
'Neath Vimy Ridge, where he, among his fellows,
Died, just as life had touched his lips to song.

And nigh as ruthlessly has life divided
Us who survive; for Abercrombie toils
In a black Northern town, beneath the glower

Of hanging smoke; and in America
Frost farms once more; and, far from The Old Nailshop
We sojourn...

Abercrombie, toiling in his "black northern town", the begetter of
the dream of Dymock, was in a way its saddest survivor. He continued to champion his theories of poetry in such books as *The Theory
of Poetry* (1924), and *Poetry, its Music and its Meaning* (1932). While at
Liverpool University in 1921, he had been invited to contribute to
The John Keats Memorial Volume, issued by the Keats House Com-
mittee and published by John Lane to mark the centenary of the
death of the poet. His essay, on 'The Second Version of Hyperion',
culminates in a poignant conclusion (The italics are Abercrombie's):

> ...We must note the extraordinary significance of the opening
> paragraph, ending with the lines —
> Whether the dream now purposed to rehearse
> Be poet's or *fanatic's* will be known
> When this warm scribe, my hand, is in the grave.
> The doubt is unresolved. Criticism is even apt to forget that it
> is Keats himself who doubts whether he has not become a
> 'fanatic'. Fanatic for what? For a vision of the world as the
> place for 'soul-making'? Something of that kind, un-
> doubtedly...

He was at Bedford College, London from 1929 to 1935, he lectured
at the University of Belfast in 1931 and in April 1935 he delivered
five lectures as a course for the Percy Turnbull Foundation at the
John Hopkins University, Baltimore on the subject of 'The Art of
Wordsworth'. The latter were posthumously published in 1952
under the editorship of his son Ralph. The Abercrombies, always
inveterate travellers, continued to indulge their passion whenever
possible. In 1931 they visited the grave of Rupert Brooke on Skyros.
An Anglo-French-Dutch group of Brooke followers had subscribed
towards a monument to Brooke to be placed high on the island.
Lascelles had been asked to give an oration in English at the afternoon ceremony. Catherine later recalled what happened next:

> When we landed from the ship in the morning, we had
> wandered away from the rest of the people, and came upon
> the tomb on a hillside with a few olive trees, and these
> shepherds sitting round a fire heating a huge cauldron of

> sheep's milk. They gave us some to drink in two-handled
> vessels that had not changed their shape since the days of
> Homer. One of them sprang to his feet and began to declaim
> a long poem which we gathered was to Rupert's memory and
> the undying friendship of English and Greeks... At their evi-
> dent request my husband spoke some Milton; as we could not
> understand a word of our different languages it did not matter
> — we were praising immortal poetry and Rupert. [TL 15
> January 1956 p.794]

As the years passed he became laden with academic honours and
honorary degrees from no less than five major universities. Yet
above all it is likely that he valued most his regular returns to speak
at the Malvern Festival annually each August. If ever there was a
coming-home, or as near as could be, it was this. And when in 1930
Oxford University Press published his *Collected Poems*, he seemed
genuinely humbled by the gesture, although in his preface he appears to have been under no illusions:

> The invitation to collect these pieces for publication...was one
> which I could not but accept with the keenest pleasure; I
> allowed it to overbear a certain unwillingness to bring
> together poems which, to me, must chiefly represent unreal-
> ized ambition.

And he meant it; as the years passed, the poetry had left him,
abandoned him rather like the dream that had ensnared him as he
had spent those first months with his sister at Much Marcle. On 27
October 1938, during his fifty-eighth year, he died in London.
Catherine had shared the gipsy fires of Ryton with him, and she lived
on to see the dream fade and die. As she said, a new generation of
poets had come, out of sympathy with the men who had seemed to
sweep all before them in the years before the First World War, who
"were determined to try new ways and thoughts and break with
tradition, and start what they thought a more significant era of
poetry — which was only to be expected after such a complete
breakdown of all that people held dear. Not that Lascelles complained. He had a serene and detached mind that helped him face
what he knew was the end of an era". And so it was, but tragically
for Abercrombie it was more personal than that. It had indeed been
a dream; it had seemed for a time to have come true, before a wider

fate betrayed it. In 1932 he had written for John Gawsworth:

> The finest curse you can put on a man is to wish him an
> ambition which he cannot attain — or, even better, which he
> can only attain to lose it again irrevocably. Mine was an
> ambition that would have harmed no one: it was but to live
> in the country and write poetry. I was not equal to it. [JG p.19]

*

Robert Frost returned to England once more, in the May and June of
1957. During this time he lectured at London University; it was an
occasion vividly remembered by Eleanor Farjeon:

> Helen Thomas and Bronwen travelled from Berkshire that
> day, and we went together to London University, where a
> small shaky lift took up to the tea-room the two old ladies who
> had somehow replaced the two active women Robert had
> known more than forty years ago. We approached a white-
> haired man who was talking to T.S. Eliot. "It's Helen and
> Eleanor, Robert." He turned towards us quickly, unmistak-
> ably Robert. Were we as unmistakably ourselves? Eliot smiled
> at us and withdrew a little. "And here's Bronnie," said Helen.
> Robert muttered, "Well, well, well." [EF/YCT p.11]

Eleanor describes the 'lecture' as having more of the feeling of an
informal chat, relaxed and without notes: "We might have been
crouched round him on the floor of Little Iddens...". Frost read his
poems — sometimes re-read them if he felt dissatisfied with the
stresses; then, holding the book with a hand that trembled slightly
but perceptibly, he said "Now I'll read you one I wrote to my friend
Edward Thomas".

On 6 June 1957 Frost came back again to Dymock. His English visit
had been full of honours — degrees conferred on him at Oxford,
Cambridge, Dublin and Durham. With him came his grand-
daughter Lesley, and a number of chroniclers and press repre-
sentatives, including Lawrance Thompson, later to write a two-
volume biography of the poet. The day before the visit to the old
lanes, after receiving his Honorary Doctorate at Oxford, he had
stayed at Shurdington on the Cheltenham to Gloucester Road in an
hotel called appropriately The Greenway. Here his old friend Jack
Haines came to see him. The next day Frost and his entourage set off
for Dymock, and were met at the rectory by the vicar, the Rev. J.E.

Gethyn-Jones. Then the sentimental journey began, first to The Old Nailshop, where Frost remarked on some of the "improvements". From there he went to Ledington, where he met an old neighbour, Harry Blandford, before hesitatingly going to his one-time home. He recognised the old water pump, and the tank near the kitchen door. He brushed the low box hedge with his hand, saying, as if to himself, "this was here when we were here". After apparently some moments of hesitation he went into the house, and wandered through its rooms. He spoke to the current owner, Mrs Causer, and smiled at her grandson Peter. Then outside, a long glance down towards Oldfields, but no more. Then he went to his last and most poignant stopping place, Ryton, to see all that was left of Abercrombie's home. The Gallows had quite simply disintegrated, and the site was marked by rubble and brambles. One overgrown wing remained, barely recognisable; the study did not exist.

It had been Frost's intention to pay one last visit to Gibson in his Surrey nursing home. Three years before he had heard that Wilfrid had little memory left. An enquiry this time told that the old man had almost completely withdrawn into his own world. It was decided against a meeting. Frost returned to America. He was a hugely celebrated figure; almost an icon now, he read at President Kennedy's inauguration in 1961. Then in January 1963, eight months after Gibson, he too died.

*

For a short span of months, a number of celebrated poets lived in and around Dymock. They walked its lanes and fields for a while, and then they went away. How important this time was for the commune itself is open to discussion; how much there really was a 'Dymock Group' is perhaps even more open to debate. In the case of the *New Numbers* enterprise, it is possible to see a strong Georgian binding of purpose; yet Frost and Thomas do not belong to that part of the story. Their mutual achievement during the Dymock time belongs to their long conversations through Kempley and Much Marcle, and down the dripping Malvern side and on the top of May Hill. It may be said that there were really two Dymock groups, and that from time to time they touched, brushed against one another before moving off again. And the influence of Frost and Thomas on the subsequent history of literature of the twentieth century and into the twenty-first is out of all proportion to the few brief sunlit months in the lanes and meadows of Dymock. When Edward Thomas's nephew Edward Eastaway Thomas formally opened the footpath that commemorated this fellowship on 27 October 1990, he drew attention to the continuing influence of his uncle in poetry, an influence directly stemming from this source:

> The path they blazed here has become literary history. Within 30 years it had prevailed over other poetic movements of the 20's and 30's. Since the end of the Second World War it has given direction to such poets as Ted Hughes, Larkin, R.S. Thomas, Sisson and others. Some critics say that without him [Edward Thomas] Heaney — and Pinter and Beckett even — would have written differently. After unveiling a memorial stone to Thomas and other Great War poets in Westminster Abbey in 1985 Ted Hughes said to me "He is the father of us all".

It cannot be disputed that Dymock had its effect on all the individuals who made up this gathering in the corner of three counties just as the world was about to go to war. In one way or another, the glow of those few months pervaded the subsequent lives, however short, of all of them. Modern weekend walkers still explore the lanes between Ryton and Greenway, and cross the fields that Frost and Thomas walked, now along well planned country footpaths, picking their way through the wild daffodils in spring, and perhaps, although they may not admit it, listen occasionally for the hint of a continuing presence somewhere just around the next bend, something persisting from those days. Landscape fed the poets; does their poetry now perhaps inform this landscape? Or then again is it just the place whispering to us as it did to them? Certainly walking through the meadows of Dymock today it is not difficult to recall that Edward Thomas once predicted our very presence here, as he passed in quiet conversation along this same path in 1914, musing on a presentiment of how one day far from his own, others would tread in his footsteps...

> ...other men through other flowers
> In those fields under the same moon
> Go talking and have easy hours.

Bibliography

Sources Quoted in the Text:

Berg FNB.   *Field Notebooks of Edward Thomas* in the Berg Collection, New York Public Library
DC   *Daily Chronicle*
EF/DB   Denys Blakelock, *Eleanor, Portrait of a Farjeon*, Victor Gollancz, 1966
EF/YCT   *You Come Too, Favourite Poems for Young Readers* Selected from his own Work and edited by Robert Frost (Foreword) The Bodley Head, 1964
EJ   Edgar Jepson, *Memories of an Edwardian and Neo-Georgian*, London, 1938
EM/CH   Christopher Hassall: *Edward Marsh*, Longmans, 1959
ET/CB   William Cooke: *Edward Thomas, A Critical Biography*, Faber & Faber, 1970
ET/GB   *Letters from Edward Thomas to Gordon Bottomley*, ed. R. George Thomas, O.U.P., 1968
ET/EF   Eleanor Farjeon: *Edward Thomas, The Last Four Years*, Faber & Faber, 1958
GP   *Green Pastures* No.2: In Memoriam Edward Thomas. Morland Press Ltd
JCT   J.C. Trewin, *Birmingham Repertory Theatre*, Barrie & Rockliff, 1963
JEW   Quoted in John Evangelist Walsh: *Into My Own, The English Years of Robert Frost*, Grove Press, New York, 1988
JG   John Gawsworth: *Ten Contemporaries: Notes Toward their Definitive Bibliography*, Ernest Benn, 1932
JH/GJ   John Haines article: 'The Dymock Poets', *Gloucester Journal*, October 1933
LML   Field Notebook in Lockwood Memorial Library, State University of New York, Buffalo
MLC   Marsh Letter Collection, Berg Collection, New York Public Library
PET   Roland Gant (ed.): *The Prose of Edward Thomas*. The Falcon Press, 1948

PP	John Drinkwater, *Prose Papers*, Elkin Mathews, 1917
PR	*Poetry Review*
PW	*Poetry Wales*, Vol 13 No 4 (Spring 1978)
RB/CH	Christopher Hassall: *Rupert Brooke, A Biography*, Faber & Faber, 1964
RB/GK	*The Letters of Rupert Brooke*, ed. Geoffrey Keynes, Harcourt, Brace & World Inc., New York, 1968
RF/LT/EY	Lawrance Thompson, *Robert Frost, The Early Years*, Jonathan Cape, 1967
RF/LT/YT	Lawrance Thompson, *Robert Frost, The Years of Triumph*, Jonathan Cape, 1971
RP	Ed. Alida Monro, *Recent Poetry 1923-1933*, Gerald Howe Ltd & the Poetry Bookshop, 1933
SLRF	*Selected Letters of Robert Frost* ed. Lawrance Thompson, Holt, Rinehart and Winston, New York, 1964
TL	*The Listener*
USW	Helen Thomas with Myfanwy Thomas: *Under Storm's Wing*, Carcanet, 1988
WHA	W.H. Auden, *Selected Essays*, Faber & Faber, 1964

Books Consulted:

Lascelles Abercrombie:
> *The Art of Wordsworth*, Geoffrey Cumberlege/O.U.P., 1952
> *The Idea of Great Poetry*, Martin Secker, 1925
> *Mary and The Bramble*, privately published, Much Marcle, 1910.
> *Poems of Lascelles Abercrombie*, O.U.P., 1930
> *The Sale of Saint Thomas*, privately published, Ryton, 1911.
> Birmingham Repertory Theatre twenty-fifth Anniversary Souvenir, 1938

Natalie S. Bober: *A Restless Spirit: The Story of Robert Frost*, Athenaeum, New York, 1981

Gordon Bottomley (ed): *An Annual of New Poetry, 1917*, Constable

Rupert Brooke:
> *Collected Poems*, (containing Marsh, Memoir) Sidgwick & Jackson, 1918
> *Letters from America*, with a preface by Henry James, Sidgwick

BIBLIOGRAPHY

& Jackson, 1916

Van Wyck Brooks: *New England: Indian Summer 1865-1915*, World Publishing, Cleveland/New York, 1946

Keith Clark: *The Muse Colony*, Redcliffe Press, 1992

William Cooke:
  Edward Thomas: A Critical Biography, Faber, 1970
  Edward Thomas, A Portrait, Hub Publications, 1978

W.H. Davies: *The Poems of W.H. Davies*, Jonathan Cape, 1940

John Drinkwater:
  Poems of Love and Earth, David Nutt, 1912
  Abraham Lincoln, Sidgwick & Jackson, 1919
  Prose Papers, Elkin Mathews, 1917
  Selected Poems, Sidgwick & Jackson, 1922

James Elroy Flecker: *Collected Poems* (with introduction by J.C. Squire), Martin Secker, 1926

Robert Frost: *Collected Poems*, O.U.P., 1951

Rev. J.E. Gethyn-Jones: *Dymock Down the Ages*, Privately Printed, 1951, republished Alan Sutton, 1951

W.W. Gibson:
  Collected Poems 1905-1925, Macmillan, 1926
  Solway Ford and Other Poems, Faber & Faber, 1945

Fay Gray Unpublished Thesis, *W.W. Gibson*

John Haines:
  'Lascelles Abercrombie: Poet', *The Gloucestershire Countryside*, Vol 3 (1937-40) pp.433-4
  'Robert Frost', *Gloucester Journal*, 15 December, 1935
  'Wilfrid Gibson', *Gloucester Journal*, 15 December, 1934
  'Edward Thomas as I Knew Him', *Gloucester Journal*

Kenneth Hare: *Gloucestershire*, Robert Hale

Alan Harfield: *Blandford & the Military*, Dorset Publishing Company, 1984

Roger Hogg: Centenary article, *Hexham Courant*, 29 September, 1978

Wilfrid Wilson Gibson: Peoples' Poet, Unpublished Ph.D. Thesis, Newcastle University Library

W.J. Keith: *The Poetry of Nature*, University of Toronto Press, 1981

Edward Marsh (ed.): *Georgian Poetry, 1911-1912*, The Poetry Bookshop, 1912

Jan Marsh: *Edward Thomas, A Poet for His Country*, Paul Elek, 1978

THE DYMOCK POETS

John Masefield:
> *The Ledbury Scene as I have used it in my Verse*. Ledbury Parish Church, 1951
> *The Collected Poems*, 1926, Heinemann

John Moore: *The Life and Letters of Edward Thomas*, Heinemann, 1939, republished Alan Sutton, 1983

Andrew Motion: *The Poetry of Edward Thomas*, Routledge and Kegan & Paul, 1980, republished 1991 by The Hogarth Press

Roy Palmer: *The Folklore of Hereford and Worcester*, Almeley: Logaston Press, 1992

David Perkins: *A History of Modern Poetry*, The Belknap Press of Harvard University Press, 1976

George Plimpton (ed.): *The Paris Review Interviews — Writers at Work*, 2nd Series, Viking (U.S.A.) 1963, Penguin, 1977

David Postle: *From Ledbury to Gloucester by Rail*, Amber Graphics, Ledbury, 1985

Michael Rathbone: *Canford School*, pub. Canford School, 1983

Timothy Rogers: *Rupert Brooke, A Reappraisal and Selection*, Routledge & Kegan Paul, 1971

Robert H. Ross: *The Georgian Revolt*, Faber & Faber, 1967

Elizabeth Shepley Sergeant: *Robert Frost: The Trial By Existence*, Holt, Rinehart and Winston, New York, 1960

Edward Eastaway Thomas: 'Opening of Poets' Path II', (Address given at Dymock, 27 October 1990) reprinted, Edward Thomas Fellowship Newsletter.

Edward Thomas:
> *The Childhood of Edward Thomas*, Faber & Faber, 1983
> *The Happy-Go-Lucky Morgans*, Boydell Press, 1983
> *The Heart of England*, O.U.P., 1982
> *In Pursuit of Spring*, Wildwood House, 1981
> *A Literary Pilgrim in England*, O.U.P., 1989
> *Richard Jefferies*, Faber & Faber, 1978
> *The South Country*, Hutchinson, 1984
> *The Icknield Way*, Constable, 1913
> *Wales*, O.U.P., 1983

Helen Thomas:
> *As It Was & World Without End*, Faber & Faber, 1972 edition
> *Time and Again*, ed. Myfanwy Thomas, Carcanet, 1978
> *Myfanwy Thomas: One of These Fine Days*, Carcanet, 1982

BIBLIOGRAPHY

(The above works by Helen and Myfanwy Thomas were published in a revised form in *Under Storm's Wing*, Carcanet, 1988)

R. George Thomas:
  Edward Thomas, A Portrait, Clarendon Press, 1985
  The Collected Poems of Edward Thomas, (ed.) O.U.P., 1981
  Letters from Edward Thomas to Gordon Bottomley, (ed.) O.U.P., 1968

Denys J. Wilcox: 'Edward Thomas, Ezra Pound and The Square Club', *PN Review*, July/August, 1992

Windcross Public Paths Project: A series of excellent and informative walk-sheets covering Dymock and the surrounding countryside

Acknowledgements

This book is the product of many friendships, and could not have been written without the goodwill and patient help of numerous people involved with, or touched by, the Dymock story in one way or another.

I am grateful to Penny Drinkwater Self, Gervase Farjeon, Lesley Lee Francis, Michael Gibson, Pam Haines, Anne Harvey, Tanya Moiseiwitsch, Edward Eastaway Thomas (nephew of Edward Thomas) and Myfanwy Thomas for valuable family insights into the poets. In and around Dymock my many friends have made my quest their own and have been unstinting in their help. Eric Bottomley, Barbara Davies, Penny Ely, Linda Hart and Roy Palmer already know of my gratitude, but it is a pleasure to record it publicly.

Jennifer Aylmer has pointed me in the right direction on several occasions, as have Fay Gray and Roger Hogg, who generously shared their knowledge of W.W. Gibson's life and work with me, while Jemma Street conducted crucial research on my behalf. Howard Moseley helped me with background to Rupert Brooke and Professor R. George Thomas clarified many points and patiently answered my queries relating to Edward Thomas. I am grateful for the guidance of a number of librarians and curators who as always have been wonderful. My thanks in this respect to Jacqueline Cox at King's College, Cambridge, Wayne Furman in the Special Collections Department of the New York Public Library, John Lancaster at Amherst College Library and Mimi Ross at Henry Holt & Company. My gratitude also to Diane Arnold at Birmingham Library Services, Peter Gilbert of The Estate of Robert Frost, Alan Harfield and Roger Pickard, past and present curators of the Royal Signals Museum at Blandford Camp in Dorset, John Stalker at Birmingham Repertory Theatre, Nigel Stewart, the librarian at Malvern College and C.R.G. Winteringham of The Sir Barry Jackson Trust.

I am grateful to Gervase Farjeon and The Estate of Eleanor Farjeon for permission to quote from Eleanor Farjeon's memoir, *Edward Thomas, The Last Four Years*. In using parts of Robert Frost's work, I acknowledge permission from The Estate of Robert Frost, Jonathan

ACKNOWLEDGEMENTS

Cape Ltd and Henry Holt & Company Inc. The Macmillan Press administer the literary estate of W.W. Gibson, and I thank them for permission to quote from his poetry. Pam Haines kindly allowed me to use extracts from the writings of John Haines, and the words of John Masefield, from 'The Everlasting Mercy' and his essay, *The Ledbury Scene as I have used it in my Verse* are reproduced by permission of the Society of Authors as the literary representative of The Estate of John Masefield. The Edward Thomas Field Notebooks are in the Henry W. and Albert A. Berg Collection, The New York Public Library Astor, Lennox and Tilden Foundations. I am grateful to have been allowed to draw on their contents. For permission to quote an extract from *Under Storm's Wing* by Helen Thomas, my thanks to Myfanwy Thomas and Carcanet Press.

Regarding photographs, and permission to use them, I must thank Pam Haines and Penny Ely for John Haines; Penny Drinkwater Self for John Drinkwater; Gervase Farjeon and Anne Harvey for Eleanor Farjeon and King's College Library for Rupert Brooke at Blandford Camp and the copy of 'The Soldier'. Pictures of Lascelles Abercrombie, and the photographs outside the old Birmingham Rep and inside the Birmingham Aluminium Works are reproduced by permission of The Sir Barry Jackson Trust and Birmingham Library Services. The photograph of Robert Frost was supplied by the Archives and Special Collections Department of Amherst College Library, and that of W.W. Gibson outside 'The Old Nailshop' was kindly loaned by his son, Michael Gibson.

Finally my thanks go to Richard Emeny of The Edward Thomas Fellowship for friendly advice and guidance, to Frank Henry, a colleague at Bournemouth University who gave his advice so willingly on matters topographical and literary, and to Christopher Somerville for walking and talking with me along the daffodil paths of Dymock in the spring of 1993. There are times in the writing of a book such as this when the research needs to be shelved for a while, and an essence rediscovered. For me that walk was just such a moment, and I began to understand something of what had happened to these writers when they found their coming together reflected by this confluence of three counties — Gloucestershire, Herefordshire and Worcestershire — in the last months before the First World War.

I have tried to contact all sources. If I have inadvertently omitted to acknowledge or thank anyone for their assistance, my sincere apologies.

Series Afterword

The Border country is that region between England and Wales which is upland and lowland, both and neither. Centuries ago kings and barons fought over these Marches without their national allegience ever being settled. In our own time, referring to his childhood, that eminent borderman Raymond Williams once said: 'We talked of "The English" who were not us, and "The Welsh" who were not us'. It is beautiful, gentle, intriguing and often surprising. It displays majestic landscapes, which show a lot, and hide some more. People now walk it, poke into its cathedrals and bookshops, and fly over or hang-glide from its mountains, yet its mystery remains.

In cultural terms the region is as fertile as (in parts) its agriculture and soil. The continued success of the Three Choirs Festival and the growth of the border town of Hay as a centre of the secondhand book trade have both attracted international recognition. The present series of introductory books is offered in the light of such events. Writers as diverse as Mary Webb, Raymond Williams and Wilfred Owen are seen in the special light — perhaps that cloudy, golden twilight so characteristic of the region — of their origin in this area or association with it. There are titles too, though fewer, on musicians and painters. The Gloucestershire composers such as Samuel Sebastian Wesley, and painters like David Jones, bear an imprint of border woods, rivers, villages and hills.

How wide is the border? Two, five or fifteen miles each side of the boundary; it depends on your perspective, on the placing of the nearest towns, on the terrain itself, and on history. In the time of Offa and after, Hereford itself was a frontier town, and Welsh was spoken there even in the nineteenth century. True border folk traditionally did not recognize those from even a few miles away. Today, with greater mobility, the crossing of boundaries is easier, whether for education, marriage, art or leisure. For myself, who spent some childhood years in Herefordshire and a decade of middle-age crossing between England and Wales once a week, I can only say that as you approach the border you feel it. Suddenly you are in that finally elusive terrain, looking from a bare height down onto the plain, or from the lower land up to a gap in the hills, and you want to explore it, maybe not to return.

This elusiveness pertains to the writers and artists too. It is often difficult to decide who is border, to what extent and with what impact on their work. The urbane Elizabeth Barrett Browning, prominent figure of the salons of London and Italy in her time, spent virtually all her life until her late twenties outside Ledbury in Herefordshire, and this fact is being seen by current critics and scholars as of more and more significance. The twentieth century 'English pastoral' composers — with names like Parry, Howells, and Vaughan Williams — were nearly all border people. One wonders whether border country is now suddenly found on the English side of the Severn Bridge, and how far even John Milton's *Comus*, famous for its first production in Ludlow Castle, is in any sense such a work. Then there is the fascinating Uxbridge-born Peggy Whistler, transposed in the 1930s into Margiad Evans to write her (epilepsis-based) visionary novels set near her adored Ross-on-Wye and which today still retain a magical charm. Further north: could Barbara Pym, born and raised in Oswestry, even remotely be called a border writer? Most people would say that the poet A.E. Housman was far more so, yet he hardly ever visited the county after which his chief book of poems, *A Shropshire Lad*, is named. Further north still: there is the village of Chirk on the boundary itself, where R.S. Thomas had his first curacy; there is Gladstone's Hawarden Library, just outside Chester and actually into Clwyd in Wales itself; there is intriguingly the Wirral town of Birkenhead, where Wilfred Owen spent his adolescence and where his fellow war poet Hedd Wyn was awarded his Chair — posthumously.

On the Welsh side the names are different. The mystic Ann Griffiths; the metaphysical poet Henry Vaughan; the astonishing nineteenth century symbolist novelist Arthur Machen (in Linda Dowling's phrase, 'Pater's prose as registered by Wilde'); and the remarkable Thomas Olivers of Gregynog, associated with the writing of the well-known hymn 'Lo He comes with clouds descending'. Those descending clouds...; in border country the scene hangs overhead, and it is easy to indulge in unwarranted speculation. Most significant perhaps is the difference to the two peoples on either side. From England, the border meant the enticement of emptiness, a strange unpopulated land, going up and up into the hills. From Wales, the border meant the road to London, to the university, or to employment, whether by droving sheep, or later to the industries of Birmingham and Liverpool. It also meant the enemy, since borders and boundaries are necessarily political. Much is shared, yet different languages are spoken, in more than one sense.

With certain notable exceptions, the books in this series are short introductory studies of one person's work or some aspect of it. There are no indexes. The bibliography lists main sources referred to in the text and sometimes others, for anyone who would like to pursue the topic further. The authors reflect the diversity of their subjects. They are specialists or academics; critics or biographers; poets or musicians themselves; or ordinary people with, however, an established reputation of writing imaginatively and directly about what moves them. They are of various ages, both sexes, Welsh and English, border people themselves or from further afield.

To those who explore the matter, the subjects — the writers, painters and composers written about — seem increasingly united by a particular kind of vision. This holds good however diverse they are in other, main ways; and of course they are diverse indeed. One might scarcely associate, it would seem, Raymond Williams with Samuel Sebastian Wesley, or Dennis Potter with Thomas Traherne. But one has to be careful in such assumptions. The epigraph to Bruce Chatwin's twentieth century novel *On the Black Hill* is a passage from the seventeeth century mystic writer Jeremy Taylor. Thomas Traherne himself is the subject of a recent American study which puts Traherne's writings into dialogue with the European philosopher-critics Martin Heidegger, Jacques Derrida and Jacques Lacan. And a current bestselling writer of thrillers, Ellis Peters, sets her stories in a Shrewsbury of the late medieval Church with a cunning quiet monk as her ever-engaging sleuth.

The vision (name incidentally of the farmhouse in Chatwin's novel) is something to do with the curious border light already mentioned. To avoid getting sentimental and mystic here — though border writers have at times been both — one might suggest literally that this effect is meteorological. Maybe the sun's rays are refracted through skeins of dew or mist that hit the stark mountains and low hills at curious ascertainable angles, with prismatic results. Not that rainbows are the point in our area: it is more the contrasts of gold, green and grey. Some writers never mention it. They don't have to. But all the artists of the region see it, are affected by it, and transpose their highly different emanations of reality through its transparencies. Meanwhile, on the ground, the tourist attractions draw squads from diverse cultural and ethnic origins; agriculture enters the genetic-engineering age; New Age travellers are welcome and unwelcome; and the motorway runs up parallel past all — 'Lord of the M5', as the poet Geoffrey Hill has dubbed the Saxon king Offa, he of the dyke which bisects the region where it can still be identified. The region has its uniqueness, then, and a statistically above-average number of writers and artists (we have identified over fifty clear candidates so far) have drawn something from it, which it is the business of this present series to elucidate.

Seven or eight poets gathered at Dymock in that brief pre-war period of 1914, and not a woman among them, apart from the underrated Eleanor Farjeon, who loved Edward Thomas and was to do much to further his renown after his death. T.S. Eliot said of the group, "These Georgians caress everything they touch", a view which encapsulates a little of what some people still feel (mistakenly) about the group's aims, and its curious, suppressed male, soft-hard, slightly askew, not entirely English quality, as the membership of Frost, Thomas and W.H. Davies indicate. Little Iddens, the cottage where Frost lived, has recently been resold, with the indirect result that a Friends of Dymock society was set up. Sean Street is its first president. His account of the Dymock poets is hardly improvable as an example of realist-narrative criticism.

The Author

Sean Street is a writer and broadcaster. He is the author of five collections of poetry, most recently *This True Making* (KQBX, 1992) and has had four plays performed in the last decade, including *Honest John* (1993) which celebrates the life of the poet John Clare. Sean Street has written books on Hampshire, Dorset, the Bournemouth Symphony Orchestra and, most recently, rural writing in *A Remembered Land* (Michael Joseph, 1994). He has produced radio programmes on W.H. Hudson, A.G. Street, Hopkins' 'The Wreck of the Deutschland' (also the subject of a book), historic farms and 'Lost Villages'. He is a regular contributor to arts and history programmes on BBC Radio 2 and 4, where his feature on Keith Douglas marked the 50th anniversary of the death of the poet in 1944.